WICCA STARTER KIT

© 2015

WICCA FOR BEGINNERS

AN INTRODUCTION TO WICCA	**10**
A Little about Real Witchcraft	11
What Most People Don't Know	11
How to Tell If It's Right For You	13
How to Get Started	14
SOME WICCAN HOLIDAYS	**16**
The Wheel of the Year	16
WICCAN GODS AND GODDESSES	**27**
The Horned God	27
The Triple Goddess	28
The All	30
The Star Goddess	30
Keep In Mind	31

BEGINNER SPELLS & RITUALS — 33

- WHAT TO KNOW — 33
- THE BEGINNING LOVE SPELL — 35
- MONEY ATTRACTION SPELL FOR BEGINNERS — 39
- GOOD LUCK SPELL — 41
- RITUAL TO BLESS WATER — 43
- A MOON RITUAL — 44

THE FIVE ELEMENTS & THEIR IMPORTANCE — 45

- AIR — 45
- FIRE — 46
- WATER — 47
- EARTH — 48
- SPIRIT — 49

THE WICCAN ALTAR & BOOK OF SHADOWS — 50

- ALTAR TOOLS — 50
- SETTING UP YOUR ALTAR — 53
- YOUR BOOK OF SHADOWS — 54

LITTLE BOOK OF SPELLS

GOOD LUCK SPELL — 58

ATTRACTING LOVE SPELL — 61

ATTRACTING WEALTH SPELL — 64

A SPELL FOR GOOD HEALTH — 67

BEAUTY SPELL — 70

HAPPINESS SPELL — 73

POWER SPELL — 76

GETTING RID OF BAD HABITS — 78

PROTECTION SPELL — 80

FINDING LOST THINGS — 83

PEACEFUL SLEEP — 85

A PEACEFUL HOME 88

ENERGY SPELL 90

CONFIDENCE SPELL 92

BIG BOOK OF SPELLS

AN INTRODUCTION TO WITCHCRAFT	**95**
A SIMPLE LOVE SPELL	**96**
CONFIDENCE SPELL & CHARM	**98**
WEEK LONG LUCK SPELL	**100**
SINGLE CANDLE MONEY SPELL	**102**
LUCK IN FINDING A JOB	**104**
A MIRROR BEAUTY SPELL	**106**
GENERAL LUCK SPELL	**108**
A BATH FOR WEALTH	**110**
A MAGICAL BAG FOR WEALTH	**112**
HOME PROTECTION SPELL	**115**

FERTILITY SPELL FOR A COUPLE	117
SPELL TO INCREASE FERTILITY	120
AN AMULET OF HAPPINESS	122
A PROTECTION POUCH	125
A GOOD DREAM POUCH	127
SAY GOODBYE TO STRESS SPELL	129
SIMPLE BANISHING POWDER	131
A SPELL TO STOP PROCRASTINATION	133
SPELL TO PURIFY AN ITEM	135
HEALING RITUAL BATH	137
A SPELL FOR HEADACHES	139
A BEDSIDE SPELL FOR HEALTH	141

DIGESTIVE HEALTH TEA SPELL	143
A SPELL FOR DECISIONS	145
HENNA TATTOO FOR ATTRACTION	148
REMOVE ENVY & JEALOUSY	150
CURSE PREVENTION POUCH	152
A BATH FOR SPIRITUAL ENERGY	154
A SPELL FOR SELF-ESTEEM	156
A GOOD LUCK COIN	159
A LITTLE ABOUT THE POWER OF BELIEF	161
ABOUT INTENT & DESIRE	163

WICCA FOR BEGINNERS

© 2015 Copyright

An Introduction to Wicca

Wicca is a peaceful way of life that teaches you to live balanced with nature, the divine, and everything that is in existence. It gives you appreciation and awe in watching the simple things, and you can enjoy nature for what it is. It is pre-Christian and it a religion that is based on the traditions of Scotland, Wales, and Ireland. Much of what Wiccans originally believed was lost because of medieval church trying to wipe Wiccans out. However, the majority of it was reconstructed, and that is what Wicca is today.

Wicca does have to do with some witchcraft, but it wasn't always seen as something evil, even though there could be evil in it. However, following the path of Wicca will take you into the light, as you're supposed to be harmonious and at peace. This doesn't have anything to do with dark spells, but instead it has to do with luck charms and relieving the stress of life by living a balanced existence.

Wicca isn't the slaughtering of animals to gain dark powers, and it certainly isn't putting a curse on anyone you don't like. Even though there can be dark spells, they aren't practiced often and they hardly ever work. When you do a spell, you are asking the Gods and Goddesses to grant you the power to do so while also harnessing the power within you.

A Little about Real Witchcraft:

Real witchcraft is a spiritual system of belief and it encourages understanding of the earth. The potion that a Wiccan stirs won't be a curse or a love brew. It'll be an aphrodisiac, cold medicine, cough syrup, or something to relieve headaches and tension. Wiccans celebrate nature, the sun cycles, the moon cycles, and the changing of the seasons. They celebrate the harmony and balance in life, and they don't worship demons or malevolent forces. They don't always try to appease a God or Goddess when they ask for their help and their guidance.

What Most People Don't Know:

What most people don't know about Wicca most of it was lost, there is no sole authority on it. There are different paths that you can take, and there are different routes you can go. There are many things that the different belief systems of Wicca hold in common, and that is what allows there to be brief guides on starting to turn to Wicca to help you find yourself. All branches hold that witchcraft is real, at least in some way.

Some believe that it comes from the Gods and Goddesses, some feel it comes from within or both, and some believe that it is all a mindset that wills things to happen. Wicca is polytheistic because there isn't just one God. It's a nature based religion, and it's considered to be an old religion at that. You're supposed to hold a deep conception and respect to all living creatures. It's considered to be a very shamanic religion, and shamanic religions are quiet similar and can be found in Asian cultures.

Wicca is primarily considered to be a branch off of Paganism. Wicca and paganism didn't have a negative connotation until Christianity started to consider it to be barbaric. Some Wiccans do not like to be associated with paganism because it's a branch that has its own set of beliefs. You have to remember that since most texts were lost, Wicca is actually a modern religion that is once again finding its roots.

There are covens in Wicca as well. This is where different people who practice get together, believing that they have more power in a number and practicing their spiritual beliefs together as a community. Different covens will choose if they are open or want to be closed because they want to make sure that you are following a similar path as them. Some will even devote themselves to a certain god or goddess.

How to Tell If It's Right For You:

There are many indications that Wicca may be right for you, and the first indication is that you aren't happy with your current religious belief. When you're looking for a new religion or to find religion for the first time, it can be extremely hard, but there are ways to tell if you lean towards one religion or another. If you're into nature, then you already going in the right direction when it comes to seeing if Wicca is a right fit.

You may lean more towards stone jewelry such as jasper pendants rather than gold or silver necklaces. You may lean more towards earthy tones rather than flashy neon colors in your wardrobe. You may find peace in nature and love animals, and this also means you might lean a little more towards Wicca than other religions.

If you prefer natural remedies, then you're more than likely going to enjoy the Wiccan path as well. In Wicca, you can learn to make your own medicine - from growing it to fixing it and you can say goodbye to headache and cold medicines. Natural remedies are part of the Wiccan way.

Wiccans are also known to remember their dreams and find importance in it, so you'll find that if you like to remember your dreams and believe they have meaning, you already share a Wiccan belief. Enjoying the outdoors is only half of the battle, but you can learn so much more about nature and living with it in Wiccan. Though some Wiccans do believe that they have psychic abilities, you don't have to have them or even truly believe in them if you want to practice Wicca.

If you're not a nature person, or you prefer medicine over natural remedies, then you're not leaning towards Wicca as a religion. You should already have an inclination towards it before you try to start, as that will make finding your way easier. The first step is to keep an open mind, and then with a little guidance you can go from there to discover and enjoy your own path.

How to Get Started:

This can be the hardest part of learning Wicca, and getting started for the first time can be hard. The first thing you need on your side is knowledge, and you'll find that this book is the path to getting started. However, you'll find that once you've gained the knowledge, you can start basic spells and practices. You can't practice Wicca if you don't know about it.

Once you've decided that the religion is for you, you're going to want to start with simple rituals and spells. Make sure that you have picked a God or Goddess you think that you can connect with, as they all stand for something else. This will help you to guide your life and become more attune with nature. It'll also be easier to find your own path and even a coven. Sometimes to start with Wicca you have to find yourself, and meditation can help you to find yourself.

When starting the most important thing to keep in mind is that you do make some of the rules and that's what helps you to choose the path you want to follow. As long as you're in tune with nature and continuously practicing, seeking peace, and trying to ground yourself, you're already working on a Wiccan path. You just need to find a personal one. Along the way you will need to gather more knowledge, tools, and spell books - including a blank journal for later use - and then you're ready to begin. You don't have to have everything at once, but you do have to be willing to expand as you go along.

Some Wiccan Holidays

The first thing you need to know is what holidays that you will be celebrating. Wiccans do not celebrate standard Christian holidays because they are not Christian, but they do have holidays and traditions of their own. You're going to need to learn about the Wheel of the Year, the Sabbats, and the Esbats. Each of these are important to following the Wiccan way of life, and each of them have to deal with nature and becoming balanced with the world.

The Wheel of the Year:

The Wheel of the Year is just a basic diagram that tells you what holidays you'll be observing and you can then get more information on them. When you're just starting out practicing you may want to keep this diagram around, as it even helps to inspire many people. There are many ways that the Wheel of the Year is represented, but it holds the same information. It tells you when all of the holidays line up, but for exact dates you'll have to look them up. Since Wiccan holidays have to deal with nature cycles, it's not the same day every single year. When you're looking at the Wheel of the Year, you'll only be seeing the Sabbats. Each are a different holiday celebrating different things.

Yule:

All Christians celebrate Christmas, but Wiccans celebrate the Sabbat called Yule. Yule falls on the winter solstice which usually falls somewhere between the twentieth of December to the twenty-third of December. It depends on when the solstice appears astronomically and that's why there isn't an exact date. The solstice is the shortest day of the year, and it is known as the longest night. It signifies that winter is coming to its end, and the days will start to grow longer again as night starts to shrink away.

It is a time that is full of feasting and there is still a gift exchange, so there is no need to worry there. Christmas was actually modified from Yule, which originated as a Pagan belief. It was a way to bring Pagans into the fold by having the Christian main holiday share similarities and be around the same time. At Yule, there is a pine tree that is decorated and burned, and it's a tradition that is meant to bring in the New Year.

Wiccans believe that this is where the Goddess gives birth to the divine god of the sun, which is why the days grow shorter. The main colors of Yule are green and purple instead of red and green at Christmas. There are many symbols of Yule - holly, mistletoe and pine are some of them. Wreaths, pine cones, and pine branches are others.

Imbolc:

Next comes Imbolc, which is in February. It can also be referred to as Imbolq, Candlemas, Brigis Day, and Bride Day. It falls around February second and is related to the mainstream holiday that is Valentine's Day. It is the celebration of the God growing in size and strength, and is related to the colors of pink and a pale green. This is distinctly different form of the green associated with Yule.

It also has many symbols that can be used and the most popular is the willow or the Candle Wheel. You'll also find that is commonly represented by Grain Dollies and Evergreens. It is the first planting of spring and you'll enjoy burning many ritual fires. It's meant to be a time of birth, inspiration and even healing. If you're going to dedicate to something or take vows, this is a popular time to do it. You can celebrate this holiday in many different ways.

You can celebrate the fertility of the Goddess Brighid, who is commonly represented by fire. Another way to celebrate is to celebrate solely the cycles of the seasons and that the planting season is upon you as the Earth is once again becoming warmed by the sun. It's a time that is meant for new beginnings and when many people choose to start a family. Many people chose to take the time of Imbolc to increase their energy and magical will power, but you don't have to. Celebrating this holiday all depends on what aspect of Wicca that you'd like to concentrate on, and that ties into your personal Wiccan path.

Ostara:

Ostara is the Spring Equinox, so it also doesn't have a direct day. In that way, it's like Yule. The Christian holiday it's related to is Easter and since its symbol is the spring flowers, there are obvious similarities between the two. It happens around the twenty-first of March, but the day will vary by a little each year. This is the time that the God and Goddess begin their courtship, and it's represented by light green. It's meant to represent the rebirth of life and it is where the dark is overtaken by the light.

It is a time where many Wiccans will meditate on their hopes and dreams because it is important to decide if you need a new beginning or if you determine you're still on the correct path. You'll be able to make changes for the year that is to come and you once again can celebrate light, fertility, and the power of the sun. It's the ushering in of spring. Agricultural changes are coming as vegetation begins to grow. It's all about finding a way to welcome the seasons and to become one with the changes that the earth is going through.

Beltane:

Beltane is next on the list, and it can also go by May Eve, Samradth, or May Day. It starts on May first. This is where the God and Goddess consummate their relationship. White, red and pink are the primary colors of Beltane. Roses are the primary flower, but spring flowers still represent this holiday as a whole. There are many fire and fertility festivals that various Wiccan covens attend or host. Many Wiccans will jump over the balefire. This practice is supposed to insure that you're protected.

Dancing around the May Pole is another significant feature of Beltane, and it is probably the most recognized practice. Bells are often rung to scare away spirits that could cause you harm. It denotes the end of spring planting. You're supposed to make sure that you take time to appreciate the affection that you have been given throughout the year. When celebrating, it usually begins the night before on the very last night of April and the celebration lasts through the entire day of May first.

The main focus is fertility, and many Wiccans may host fertility parties, but there is no reason to do so if you feel uncomfortable with that practice. The union of the God and Goddess is supposed to bring about a good crop and healthy, strong livestock. Like most Wiccan holidays, you're supposed to celebrate Beltane your way, and you don't have to do anything that you don't want to. There are no requirements other than the appreciation of the crops that are to come.

Litha:

Litha is next holiday and it is also called the Summer Solstice or Midsummer. Summer is in full swing by now, and your gardens should be in full bloom when this Wiccan holiday comes around on the Wheel of the Year. Since it is the solstice, you'll find that the day does change by the year, but it is usually around June twenty-first. This is where the Goddess is pregnant with the God and that is what is being celebrated. White and pale yellows are the color of Litha.

Litha is the longest day of the year and therefore it has the shortest night. The cauldron and the spear are both common symbols. Other symbols include birch, St. John's Wort (which has many medicinal properties), and white lilies. It's considered to be the peak of magical power because it is the peak of the sun. You're mean to celebrate abundance.

Many people celebrate fertility at this point as well. Virility, beauty, and the bounty that the earth brings you is also celebrated on Litha. Consummation and empowerment are the main themes of this holiday, and often large bonfires are lit after sundown during any Wiccan celebration of this holiday. The main point of Litha is to celebrate nature and try to connect with it, so meditation is also involved. You should spend Litha outdoors.

Lammas:

Another common name is Lanasa, but it also goes by Lughnasad. Gold and bright yellows are the colors that are associated with it. The date of Lammas is August first and it doesn't change depending on the year. Nuts, grains, and the summer flowers are the symbols of Lammas. It denotes the first grain harvest and a feast is usually dedicated to the Mother. It is also a celebration of death, as the cycle of life is completed. It's a time that all Wiccans are supposed to take note of their blessings. A fire and light festival is usually practiced.

There is an abundance in the fall months and Wiccans are supposed to reflect on that. You have to recognize at this time that summer will soon be at its end. Apples and grapes are usually ripe at this time, and they are often prominently featured in the festivals that are to come because of it. It's a time to be grateful for the little things, including the food that is on your table both that night and for the nights to come.

Mabon:

Mabon is around September first, but it's not on the same day every year because it's the Autumn Equinox. It's also referred to as the Pagan or Wiccan Thanksgiving. Many refer to it as the Harvest Home. At this point the God is considered to be sleeping in the womb of the Goddess, also known as the mother. The colors that represent it are a dark brown and a rich red. Its symbols are the harvest foods that many enjoy.

Mabon is considered to be the second harvest festival and it's a festival where you once again have a feast, giving thanks to the crops that you've been able to sow. The darkness is once again overtaking the light and it needs to be recognized in the

Wiccan religion. Honoring the changing seasons is very important when you're trying to connect to nature. It's a time where you should be thankful for other things in your life as well, and you have to accept that the soil is dying and there will not always be an abundance. The winter is known to be hard months. You have to realize that the cold is what is ahead, but you can handle it and it is nothing to fear.

Samhain:

This is the last holiday before you celebrate Yule again. It is related to Halloween, and this is when the fields have grown bare. Oranges and brown represent it and it is on the thirty-first of October. It's often referred to as Summer's End, All Hollow's Eve, or the Witches' New Year. Fall fruits represent it and it is the day where you have to respect that the worlds of the living and the dead are closer than ever.

Many Wiccans will take this as an opportunity to practice their divination to help guide them in the future. To celebrate this day where the dead are closer to the living, you are supposed to set a place for the loved ones that passed at your table, welcoming them and remembering them. Other Wiccans will set out food and drink outside of their door as an offering to the spirits as they roam. It's to help the souls that are still wandering until the veil becomes thick once more. Again, you're celebrating death and rebirth. You are meant to honor those have died and remember your ancestors. If you wish to contact the dead, this is considered to be the perfect time.

The Esbats:

Esbats have to deal with the moon cycles, and they are when many covens will meet up and practice together. If you don't belong to a coven, you can still harness the power of the Esbats by practicing spells on these nights or just strengthening your sense of self. You start with the full moon and go through the moon phases. Each phase is used for something different, but each phase has its own type of power.

Full Moon:

You start with the full moon, which is supposed to be one of the most powerful nights in the cycle. If you need to do a banishing spell, it is best to do it on this night. You can also use it for protection spells and it will help with divination on a monthly basis as well. You don't always have to wait for Samhain.

Some Wiccans believe that it is a seven day window that you can use, but the night when the moon is full in the sky is the most powerful. Three days before the full moon and three days after is the only window. There are some spells that can only be created in this full cycle.

New Moon:

As a Wiccan, you can't forget the power of the New Moon either. This is a time that is meant for personal growth and it is a great day for healing. If you need to heal yourself emotionally or try to increase your physical healing rate, the New Moon is the best time. Blessings are best at this time, as well as personal ventures. You may not see the results of these spells until the next full moon, as it can take a full cycle to complete this type of magic.

Waxing Moon:

The waxing moon is a time to attract things and many Wiccans use this time to attract wealth. It can help to give you luck in any business venture if the right spell has been put into motion. A good luck bag is also made under the waxing moon, as it's more likely to draw the luck to you. It's also a time to help with relationships because you can attract your partner to you. Many aphrodisiacs are brewed under the waxing moon.

Waning Moon:

Banishing and rejecting is meant to take place on the waning moon, so you need to tread carefully in relationships and new ventures. However, you can use this as a time of cleansing. You can get rid of negative spirits and negative energy in your life. You can make the changes necessary to be more positive, kick bad habits, and cleanse your body of diseases and aliments. Some Wiccans choose to brew herbal remedies that are meant to help with cravings or common ailments such as the cold under the waning moon.

The Dark of the Moon:

The time before a New Moon is considered the dark of the moon. It happens in a three day window before the New Moon, and at this time you are meant to rest and recuperate. You should not perform magic at this time, as it isn't known to work properly. Vision quests and meditations are often performed at this time, but you shouldn't do so for magical purposes. It should be used to realign you to your past. There is only one time that you will perform magic in this three day window, and that is if you are looking for guidance from Hekate, as she rules over this period of time.

Wiccan Gods and Goddesses

There are main Gods and Goddesses no matter which path you are on in Wicca, and there are ways that they need to be worshipped or at least acknowledged. You cannot acknowledge them if you do not know who they are and before practicing you need to at least know the basics. When you feel that you're connected to one or the other, you're more likely to turn to this God or Goddess in times of great need or trouble.

The Horned God:

Since this god is named the "Horned God", many fear that it is related to the Christian devil, but this is not the case at all. The Horned God was a concept long before the Christian concept of Satan, and actually in the bible it does not describe Satan as having horns or even hooves. These descriptions were added in the middle ages to keep people in fear of Pagan and Wiccan culture. What most people misconstrue is that the Horned God is not one God, but there are many Horned Gods that could hear you calling out to them.

Other Wiccans will believe that there is only one. The base of the Horned God is that it encompasses all masculine traits. They are often depicted as a satyr - God's that have the bottom half of a ram or a goat. They are also known, quite obviously, for their conical horns. Sometimes they are depicted as having animal heads or having goat hooves.

It really depends on the path that you're following and which texts you are going to believe. It's meant to represent the wild or primal nature that can be found within a man. It is meant to be a man, or rather a God, which is not leashed by civilization or society. It is a God that has a wild side, living by instinct and in a natural state. They are often said to be found in forests, and they are connected to the hunt.

The virility of men is also represented by the Horned God. The Horned God is known to embrace his sexual desires, unlike where society asks that is leashed and tamped down. There are versions of the Horned God that are different, but these are the main themes. There are many Wiccans that will worship the Horned God, but it may not be the same one.

The Triple Goddess:

The Triple Goddess is represented by three figures, and it is often the three stages of womanhood. The Maiden comes first, and she is the young and innocent version of the Triple Goddess. Often, she is depicted as a virgin, but this is not necessary. She is always depicted as beautiful. She is meant to be independent, and usually is ready to take on the world.

She is open to future possibilities and she looks to what promises there can be in the world. The maiden represents a woman's youth. She also represents new beginnings, the new moon, and spring fertility festivals.

Next comes the Mother who is considered to be mature, and she's also known to have a lot of sexuality. The Mother is said to be an experienced lover, and she is usually shown as a parent, but this too isn't set in stone. She's a protective and nurturing form of the Triple Goddess. She has selfless traits, and she is still full of sexuality. She sustains others, and she is often involved in domestic issues, growth, the full moon, and summer. She gets pregnant in the summer and gives birth in the winter.

The third side of the Triple Goddess is the Crone, and she is the wise part of the Triple Goddess. You go to her for guidance, and she is considered to be an elder that is respected, and often she is depicted as a grandmother. She's pragmatic and doesn't lack in strength. She is the dark side, and she represents the fear of aging, destruction, decay as well as fears in general. She is not evil in the least, but she will guide you through the challenges in life, and she does represent death and rebirth.

The most important thing to remember about the Triple Goddess is that she is meant to represent the feminine aspects. She is the life stages of a woman and she is meant to be wise and strong throughout. She is independent and so she can depend on herself instead of being forced to depend on a man. You can celebrate one part of the Triple Goddess in certain Wiccan holidays or even paths without celebrating the others. It is just more common to celebrate all three.

The All:

Also known as The One, this is another primary deity in Wicca, and you'll find that it's often the hardest to understand. This deity is considered to be unknowable, unlike the others that are worshipped. It should not be confused with Wicca being monotheistic because it is not, and it does not mean the same thing. It's also important to keep in mind that in Wicca nature is also meant to be divine itself, so it is not nature either. It is considered to be an ultimate deity as well as an impersonal one, and that is the reason it is not worshipped. It will not intervene, and it is not believed that it will help you. So you do not come to this deity for anything. Not even rituals or spells.

The Star Goddess:

The Star Goddess is yet another Goddess in Wicca, and she can often be called "God Herself". She is one of the main goddesses in Feri, which ties into a Wiccan path. She is considered to be the darkness in deep space which is primal, and she is considered to be what makes the void intelligent. She is considered often to have created everything that you see around you, but that is a debatable point depending on what path you are going with on Wicca.

However, when starting Wicca it is important that you know about her and decide what parts you do and do not believe in. she often has a halo of flames around her in many depictions, but it others she doesn't quite look human. She can be seen as having wings, and other depictions have her with the head of a black lion. She can also be represented by a serpent eating its own tail.

Keep In Mind:

What you need to keep in mind is that these are not the only Wiccan gods and goddesses, and there are many others that you may ask for help. At one point or another you may worship many of them, looking for guidance or a solution to a problem. There is a god or goddess out there for almost everything that you could need, but usually you will connect to one in particular.

There's still the Death Goddess which is self-explanatory, and there is the Great Mother Goddess which represents a heaven like Goddess. You'll find that there are other spirits that can be important as well that aren't necessarily deities, and there are evil spirits in Wicca as well, which you are supposed to protect yourself against.

Beginner Spells & Rituals

When you're going to be practicing Wicca there will be a few spells that you will eventually cast as well as rituals, and in this chapter you'll find beginner spells. Spells aren't as hard as they sound, but you do need the right tools if you plan to do them right. Beginner spells don't usually require too many materials, but those that do have such a long list because they don't require as much skill or work due to what you're putting into it.

What to Know:

Before you can cast any spells there are a few basic concepts of Wicca that you have to understand, and the first thing is that everything in Wicca has an essence. It is a type of force that runs through all things, including stones. It is what gives objects and people their power. It is what makes blood so potent, and it is what allows you to cast anything at all. No matter how simple. An essence is actually a part of the divine that runs through everything, and it is seen as what connects us to everything in the world, including but not limited to nature as a whole.

The next thing you need to know is that energy work is considered magic in Wicca. There are some branches of

Wicca that don't consider all energy work to be magic, but the majority does. It doesn't matter if you're preforming a religious rite, casting a spell or just a circle for one reason or another. It is not required as a Wiccan to practice spell casting, but it is abnormal not to do so.

You also need to realize that magic doesn't mean miracle, and it does have limitations and uses. You can't just do whatever you want and expect it to work. Magic only comes with hard work and dedication. It also comes with faith and belief. Without that, you will not accomplish anything at all no matter how good the spell is. You can get results that are not what you expected either. Sometimes the results aren't as potent or visible as you want them to be, but that is the will of the world. It is not just your will that matters.

Magic also works better on you than other people. If you're trying to get help with something that has to deal with you, you are more likely going to succeed. If you are trying to use magic to affect other people, it is still possible but much more unlikely and much less potent. You have to believe though. Without faith, nothing will happen at all. It's often written off as psychological because of it, and that's partially right. Part of it is psychological, but you cannot release your inner energy or tap into something else's energy if you don't believe that you can. You'll be setting up mental blocks that will cause you to fail at whatever your goal is.

Not all spells have to be cast with a certain deity in mind, but you do need to remember that most do. When you cast in the name of a particular deity, you can't expect them to take care of everything. You still have to put in the work, but you're just casting it either asking for help or to honor the deity of your choice. Now that you know all of these little tidbits and facts about spell casting, you're more than likely ready to learn as you go and try a few things out. Beginner spells are always best, and then you can move onto performing rituals and beginner rituals.

The Beginning Love Spell:

Don't let the name fool you. This isn't something that is going to create long lasting love with the person of your dreams. You can't snag a celebrity or hope to create a marriage based on it. This spell is for attraction, pure and simple. At best it will create a mild obsession, but this beginning spell should open the gateway you need to have a relationship with someone that you want to have one with.

Don't bother with keeping a particular person in mind because it just won't help because this is a zero ingredient spell. It requires your own energy and the energy and blessing of nature around you. A mantra will need to be repeated, but first you need to start with an everyday routine. Start by taking time to meditate every single day. You'll need to just sit there and concentrate on the type of person that you want to attract. Not the who, but the what.

Visualizing a person that would encompass what you want will also help, as you need to visualize to bring everything into being or rather into reality. You may need to do this spell once every month, and it may take time for it to kick in since there are no ingredients. This spell is to be performed under the full moon. Do not try under any other moon, as it will not have enough power.

The mantra you'll be repeating goes as follows:

"Brilliant moon at this hour, I call upon your magic power. Give to me the love I seek. As I will it, so mote it be."

This isn't a particularly strong mantra, and as a beginning Wiccan it is not best to change it. You can make it a little more personal as you gain skill and knowledge. You also need to remember that it doesn't need to rhyme, but it should be something that you can remember. If you can't remember it and speak from the heart, don't expect it to work. There won't be any power behind it.

Love Spell with Ingredients:

This love spell is still for beginners, but it does require ingredients. It's also performed on the full moon. Luckily, the ingredients for this spell are considered easy to find, and there aren't that many of them to worry. Just remember that quality of your ingredients in a Wiccan spell is known to make a difference.

Ingredients:

- 2 Red Candles
- 3 White Candles
- Rose Petals
- Special Jewelry

Now before you move onto directions, you need to know that some people believe that pink candles will work as well. However, it is usually best to stick with the basic red for love instead. The quality of your rose petals will also make a difference. You may not want store bought rose petals if you can help it because you don't want the preservatives that are put on most rose petal boxes.

Gathering your own is best, and try for red if possible. If not, a pink will do, but do not use any other color. You are also probably wondering why you need the jewelry, but the jewelry is your base and it is what the spell will be centered around. It can be as simple as a charm that you put on a bracelet or necklace.

Directions:

1. You'll need to take a knife to carve into the candles, so make sure they aren't in glass containers that you can't get them out of. Carve a heart into them to begin.

2. You're going to then lay out the rose petals in a pentacle design. The red candles will be your first and secondary elements, and the white will represent the other three.

3. The charm should be placed at the center, and then you will light the candle starting with the first element, then the secondary and go around until they are all lit.

4. The mantra is really simple. "Five candles lit by the Full Moon, let true love arrive to me soon."

5. You should repeat this three times before meditating while the candles burn out on their own for the best effect. Remember to do this on a full moon and a full moon only.

Money Attraction Spell for Beginners:

This is an older type of spell, and it is very similar to many Pagan spells, but it is Wiccan. You can't expect to get wealthy off of this spell, but it is meant to bring you better luck in your financial endeavors. The potency of this spells depends on the person and how much they're willing to put into it. It will also take time for this spell to actually start working, but you at least only need two ingredients to get started.

Ingredients:

1. 1 Green Candle
2. 13 Inches of Green Silk

Directions:

1. You're going to start by making a knot and repeating the first line of the spell. "With knot one, it has begun."

2. Another knot. "Then with two, there's work to do."

3. Another knot. "With knot three, money shall come to me."

4. Another knot. "With knot four, opportunity journeys to my door."

5. Another knot. "With knot five, there's no doubt I will thrive."

6. Another knot. "With knot six, money problems are fixed."

7. Another knot. "With knot seven, success will start to happen."

8. Another knot. "With knot eight, increasing it is great."

9. Another knot. "With knot nine, all of it is mine."

Remember to do this spell on the waxing moon because it will help you to attract things. You'll get your best results here, but if you try it on the waning moon it may not work at all or even just backfire on you. Moon cycles are important, so always be patient and pay attention to when the time is right.

Good Luck Spell:

Everyone could use a little better luck, and this is also a spell that you'll want to do on a waxing moon and not a waning moon. Only use the waxing moon if you are trying to banish bad luck. It's not that many ingredients and they're rather inexpensive, so it's the perfect spell for beginners.

Ingredients:

1. 1 Black Candle
2. Frankincense Oil

Directions:

1. You aren't supposed to light the candle yet, but instead pour the frankincense oil on your fingertip, and streak the candle. You should do this three times while repeating the next line. "Black candle, let's turn my luck around. Bring to me prosperity and joy abound."

2. Now you'll need to light the candle after thanking it. Remember that everything has an essence. Your hand needs to be placed on your heart chakra as you repeat, "Flame and fire, candle burn. Work and make my luck return."

3. You'll need to use visualization as you chant to help bring it into reality. You should keep chanting, letting it lift

you up and fill you with positivity, until you feel you're done. Then you should softly blow the candle out.

Ritual to Bless Water:

This water is going to go in your chalice, and most Wiccans put the blessed water on their Altar for later use. It helps you to purify negative energy later, and it'll keep out this negative energy when you're doing a ritual. You should use natural water, so don't just buy spring water if you can help it. If you can obtain it from a running spring or creek it is best. Blessing water is actually a very simple beginner ritual.

Directions:

1.	Place the water inside the chalice, and then put your hand over the water.

2.	Repeat this prayer to the God and Goddess in order for them to bless the water.

"Divine Father, Mother Goddess, please purify this water with your divine powers. Bless it with your light."

3.	Add salt to the water while blessing it, as it'll help to purify the water as well.

You need to remember that every once in a while this water will need to be replaced. You can't just always have stale water sitting around. However, it's disrespectful if you just pour it down the drain. Let it go back to the earth, and you can use it as an offering at the foot of a tree.

A Moon Ritual:

This is best to perform on the full moon, but you can perform it on almost any moon as well. You're going to be recharging yourself, which will give you more magical energy to work with on any other spell or ritual. Just make sure you have your wand with you. The athame should work as well.

Directions:

1.   Start by blessing the area. You can take your chalice with the blessed water and sprinkle it around in a circle.

2.   Then draw the circle with your athame or wand. Sit directly in the circle under the moonlight.

3.   Meditate for thirty minutes. It's best to occasionally repeat the mantra below.

"Gods and Goddesses please give me the energy I need to do what is right. Please allow me to be guided by your wisdom. I ask that you accept me into your fold."

The Five Elements & Their Importance

There is more to the five elements in Wicca than just knowing their name, and there is a lot that they represent. There is also a lot that these elements can be represented by in rituals and spells. You need to understand the five elements fully if you want to practice Wicca even without the spells and rituals. When you do add those in, it will be more complicated. Understanding these elements completely will be essential if you ever want to modify a spell or ritual or even create your own.

Air:

Air can represent a lot of different thing, including telepathy, psychic powers, communication, ideas, knowledge, and the mind as well as intelligence. It can also represent wishes and dreams, as well as your inspiration and imagination. Aromatherapy can be a representation, as well as tossing something into the wind, singing, and putting something in a high place. Air is also represented in visualization.

It has the direction of East, and it is naturally masculine. It has projective energy and is found in the upper left of the pentagram. When you're looking for a symbol of air, clouds, wind, smoke, herbs, trees, flowers, and feathers are most commonly used. The best time when dealing with the element air in something is dawn, and in the cycle of life it is infancy. Its season is the spring, and it has crimson, white and yellow as its colors.

Topaz, pumice, crystals, amethyst, rainbow stones and alexandrite are the jewels and stones that represent it. You'll usually use the wand, censer or sword to represent it in a ritual. The raven and eagle are often representatives of air. The flute represents air as well.

Fire:

Fire is meant to represent energy, but it also is meant to represent love, passion, inspiration and even leadership. You'll bring objects in rituals to represent it, and it relates to love spell rituals, baking, and in rituals you'll represent fire by lighting fires and candles. Fire is meant to man change, but it also represents raw magic, and it is one of the most physical elements. It is also masculine in gender, and the direction is south. It has projective energy, and it's on the lower right of the pentagram.

It is meant to represent youth in the cycle of life, and the season for fire is summer. The colors for fire are gold, orange, white, red and crimson. If you are representing fires with stones, you'll usually use ruby or volcanic lava. However, you can also use agate and fire opal. It can be represented by the cat, snake, or dragon. The metals for fire are gold and brass, and herbs for fire include garlic, cinnamon, red peppers, and seeds.

Water:

Water is actually feminine and it has receptive energy. It's commonly represented by the lake, rain, wells, rivers or oceans. However, it can also be represented by shells, cups, and fog. It represents your emotions, subconscious, and your soul. It also means wisdom, eternal movement, absorption, and the emotional side of femininity and love.

When you need to represent water in rituals you'll usually pour it over objects, heal with it, use ritual bathing, toss objects into water, or even in brew making. The direction for water is west. It's the upper right of the pentagram. It is maturity in the cycle of life, and its season is autumn. The best time for water based rituals is at twilight or dusk.

The colors for water are green, grey, black, indigo, and shades of blue. When you're using stones, you'll want to use pearl, fluorite, blue topaz, coral, and aquamarine. Magic tools for it are goblets, mirrors, cups and cauldrons. If you need a metal, you'll need to use either copper or silver. It can also be represented by water snakes, dolphins, fish, and turtles. Another animal is the swan or crab. If you need herbs to represent it you'll use the lotus, mosses, water lilies or gardenia. It's best for lucid dreaming, protection, cleansing, and mirror divinations.

Earth:

Earth is also feminine, and the direction for it is north. It also has receptive energy, and it helps to represent abundance, stability, wealth, prosperity, and strength. When using it in rituals, you'll find that you usually bury an object, use herbalism, or make images out of stone or even wood. It's placed on the lower left of the pentagram.

Common symbols are rocks, soil, salt, clay and caves. The best time to perform earth magic is at night, especially midnight. It is the age in the cycle of life, and the season for earth is winter. If you need to represent it by colors you can use yellow, brown, green or black. Green is the most common. When you need stones, you'll want emerald, onyx, salt, quarts, or jasper.

The tools that are related to earth in your rituals are the salt, stones, ems, cords, and pentagram. If you need a metal you'll have to use iron or lead. Iron is much easier to get ahold of, and for herbs ivy, grain, rice, or oats work well. However, lichens and patchouli will also do the trick. Cows, bears, and wolves usually represent it in animal form.

It's great for stone magic, knot magic, binding, grounding, runes, gardening, and money spells. Burying, planting, or cutting herbs are ritual actions that relate to it. Earth is also related to making anything out of clay while in your circle. It's a common element to use simply because of the protection and grounding purposes that it serves.

Spirit:

This is the last element, and it's the top of the pentagram. It's universal in gender, types of energy, and direction. The symbols are cords and ropes. It represents the eternal, and the color for it is white. It is what connects you to the other elements, and it represents both joy and union. The animal that represents it is the dove.

The Wiccan Altar & Book of Shadows

Both the Wiccan Altar and book of shadows is extremely important. With your Altar you'll be able to do more than just basic spells, but rituals are for more than just beginners. It will help you become more versed in Wicca, and your book of shadows is something that you will eventually be able to pass down. So make sure to watch your handwriting, and make sure that everything you get is quality, as it'll affect your ability to practice.

Altar Tools:

Before you start with a Wiccan ritual, you first need to learn about ritual tools. You will not need all of these tools for every ritual, but you should familiarize yourself with all of them in the case that they're needed for future rituals. For example, there is a special knife that you use in Wiccan rituals called an athame.

It is not used for cutting, but is meant to direct spiritual energy as you need it to. This is why you'll find that many athames are rather dull, but they do have a dual edge. The handle is always dark and traditionally it is black. It can be intricate or simple, and that really depends on your preference. It's linked to the fire element, and they are often representatives of the God in Wicca, usually the Horned God, and this is because of their phallic shape.

The Boline is another knife that is used for cutting. However, it usually is only meant to cut cords, wands, inscribing symbols, or cutting herbs. It can be used outside the circle as well as inside, and it doesn't have to be a fancy blade. You just need to make sure that it is kept sharp and clean. Clean it well after each and every ritual, and do not let it start to rust.

Cauldrons are also often needed, and it is great for brewing. It is meant to symbolize transformation, but it can also be used to symbolize fertility as well as femininity. It's connected to water and the Goddess. It can be the focal point of a ritual, and it should have three legs. Make sure that it's made of cast iron for the best cauldron. It has a multipurpose nature, and this is incredibly useful, so invest in your cauldron.

You'll also need a besom, which is considered to be a witch's broomstick. However, it's a myth that they're used for flying. It is meant to cleanse an area, but only symbolically. It will also help to take out negative energies before a ritual. You should use it after a ritual to make sure the negative energies are taken out as well. Usually they should be made of willow binding, birch twigs, with an ash staff. However, if you can't get ahold of that, you just need to make sure that you make your besom out of only natural material.

The chalice is also important, and it is very similar in purpose to the cauldron. However, it has a much smaller capacity. It can be used to hold salt water to help cleanse an object, ritual wine or other liquids, or just used to mix potions. It symbolizes the Goddess of fertility, and it is related to the element of water.

The censer is next, and it is an incense burner that is ceremonial. You should put your incense here during the ritual, but any bowl or cup can be used if necessary. Breathing in a burning incense is meant to help you Altar your consciousness to where it needs to be for a ritual. It is often placed on an altar, and it connects with the air element.

Crystals are also important, but you won't know what crystals you need until you know what ritual or spell that you'll be performing, as they are used in both. It is best to get them as you need them or when you see them for a good price without needing to sacrifice quality. Start collecting stones, as you'll find that they prove useful later on.

You'll also need a pentacle that is on a flat disc. It is meant to be a symbol, and it should be a five pointed star with a circle around it. It can be made of any material. You can even have it made out of wood, clay or even wax. However, many people prefer it on brass, gold, copper or silver. It is meant to help to protect you and it's used for invocation. It can help you by acting like a portal between our world and the world of the spirits.

The wand is also needed, and it has been used since Paganism. It directs energies, helps you to create magical symbols and draw circles. It is linked to air, and it is a cared element. They are usually made from willow, oak or elder. Crystals can be added to the tip to amplify the energy. You'll need a book of shadows next to read from, but you'll be creating that yourself later on.

Setting Up Your Altar:

Start by putting it somewhere that won't be disturbed. It is best to keep you Altar in a separate room, and some people use walk in closets. You already know all of the items that go into your Altar, but a stone table is usually best. However, a wooden table will also work. Set up all of your items the way you like them, and make sure that you have blessed the objects with blessed water, which you've already learned the ritual for. Some people put a theme to it based on color, but it is usually best to keep it blank so that it worships all elements and both the God and the Goddess.

Your Book of Shadows:

A book of shadows is essential when you're practicing Wicca. This is a journal that you use to store information for your spells, rituals, and magical traditions. A book of shadows should always be handwritten, so it shouldn't just be stored on the computer. It's considered a sacred tool, so if you don't hand write it, then you aren't showing it the respect you need to.

It's going to be an item of power, and you'll want to keep this on your Altar as well. By writing in your book of shadows it also helps you to memorize the spells and rituals a little more, and it will transfer energy to you. Just make sure to take time. Never write in your book of shadows if you don't have the time because it should be written in ink. There will not be a second chance to write it in.

You'll be reading your notes during different spells and rituals, especially when you get to advanced ones, as they're much longer. A leather journal is traditional, but some people have used a three-ring binder. Make sure to keep your book of shadows clean, and it should be read by you and those you trust. No one else.

Some people take it a step further by coding their book of shadows, but this isn't something you should do unless there are rituals that you think are too dangerous. There's no reason to put anything in the book of shadows that you don't want to. You can even write notes in your book of shadows on how to make spells and rituals more powerful.

However, even though it's your book, there are a few things that are expected to be in it. You'll need a dedication at the beginning, and it's not a normal book dedication. Instead it's who you've dedicated yourself to. Usually it's a God or Goddess, as you dedicate yourself to them usually before a coven. However, if you joined a coven first, you'd put down a copy of your initiation.

You'll also need to put down a correspondence table under each spell. This tells you what you used your tools for. For example, since green can represent different elements, you'd have to put why you used it. This will help you to repeat spells and rituals without mistakes as needed. You'll also want to put down Sabbat rituals and even some esbats rituals.

In the back you'll put what you learn about specific herbs that you use often, magical recipes, and anything you want to pull from a sacred text and reference often. It's also important to put down power mantras as you need them and find them. A book of shadows is primarily for rituals, but you can put spells in here as well. If you choose to keep spells separately, they'll go in a book called a grimoire. It is usually best to make it out of a leather bound journal as well.

Now you know everything you need to get started with Wicca, and as you go along you'll be adding to your book of shadows and grimoire. Make sure that you start with basic spells and rituals, building your skill over time. The more you understand about Wicca the more power you'll have.

LITTLE BOOK OF SPELLS

© 2015

Good Luck Spell

Everyone can use a bit of luck, and this twenty-four hour luck spell is sure to do the trick. You can use it to find success, happiness, and even financial gain. It's completely up to you and the energy that you put into it. You'll start by reaching a meditative state the night before, so make sure that you do it on the right day.

Ingredients:

1. 1 White Candle
2. White Sage Smudge Stick
3. 1 Wooden Bowl

Directions:

1. Start by lighting the candle in front of you after sitting down with your legs crossed. You should be outside and under the full moon. Keep your eyes closed.

2. Light the sage and then move it around you slowly before placing it back in the bowl.

3. You need to concentrate on your breathing. Breathe in and out until you reach a meditative state, and then you can

open your eyes. Look up to the moon. If there is cloud, don't worry.

4.   Repeat the following chant: "Dianna, Goddess of the Moon, I ask that I am granted luck. I ask that you guide me in my endeavors. I ask that you may grant me your gift of success and positive surprises. Please allow me to see your light."

5.   Say this three times before going back to meditation. Put out the candle and sage before going back inside.

Best Time to Do It:

It's always best that you do this under the full moon, but any moon except for the New Moon will work. There is no light on the New Moon, and you can open yourself to negative energies in the dark. The sage will help with this, but it is still not recommended. It's important that you do this around midnight, as that is the best time for spells to take effect.

Why Use These Ingredients:

You're going to want to use white sage because it purifies you and the area. A smudge stick is just easier, but if you have loose sage, it works just as well. It can just be difficult if you're trying to keep it burning without it being bundled together. The white candle is also meant to show purity, and it's meant to represent spirit energy, which will be needed to help to improve your luck. Do not use a different candle color, or you'll be opening yourself up to negative energies that can ruin your spell.

Attracting Love Spell

Everyone wants a love spell here and again, but they're easier said than done. It's important to remember that attraction is a little easier than forcing someone to love you, which many people find to be impossible. It's best that you use this with a charm, as it'll help to attract wherever and whenever you go.

Ingredients:

1. 1 Sterling Silver Ring
2. 1 White Cloth
3. Spade
4. White Wine

Directions:

1. You'll want to go outside, and it's best to do this on property that you won. So try to find the bottom of a tree that is graced by moonlight. If not, just make sure that the moon is shining that night and kneel on the ground.

2. You'll want to look up and repeat the chant. "Blessed Goddess of the Moon, honest and true, here's a silver gift that I offer to you. Please bless this ring, please make it shine. Please give me a lover to be truly mine."

3.   Now wrap the ring in the white cloth, and bury it at the foot of the tree or in the earth. Cover it back with dirt, and then take the wine, pouring it over the ground as a further offering.

4.   You'll need to leave it until the next full moon. Then unbury it, and pour more white wine over the hole after it's been recovered.

5.   You can then wear the ring either on your finger or around your neck on a chain. It's important to have it on you as much as possible to attract a mate.

Best Time to do This:

The best time is a full moon, as you'll be able to get the Goddess's attention that much easier. You can do this on a half moon, but it will not be nearly as powerful. It is important that you do wait an entire lunar cycle before pulling it back up. It is best to do this at the end of winter, as it shows rebirth, and it'll help you to grow the love that you want between you and your future mate.

Why These Ingredients:

White wine is more pure than red wine. Red wine often symbolizes blood, which you don't need in this type of spell. You'll need to offer it as a gift to the Goddess. Sterling silver is asked for just because it is the purest silver that you can get ahold of, and it can be seen as an offering as well. It works well with taking on energies, and a white cloth is to make sure that the item stays pure when put into the ground, allowing the Goddess to bless it. If you do not have white wine, you can use blessed water, but it is not known to be as effective.

Attracting Wealth Spell

If you're struggling with finding wealth, there's no way to make sure that you win the lottery, but you can attract more wealth to you over time. You have to be willing to put the time and energy into it, but this spell will help. This money magnet spell will help you to get more money over time, and it's easy to gather the ingredients for it. Just make sure that you don't substitute anything.

Ingredients:

1. 1 Silver Bowl
2. 1 Cinnamon Stick
3. 1 Piece Malachite
4. Pine Essential Oil
5. Dried Dill

Directions:

1. Take the silver bowl, and add in the cinnamon stick as well as the dill.

2. Next, you're going to want to add the pine oil and stir with your finger. Do not use anything else to stir.

3. The malachite will then need to be placed in the bowl. Make sure it is covered completely by the herbal mixture.

4. This should be done on your altar, and you'll need to leave it in this mixture for seven days.

5. Afterwards, you'll take the malachite out, and carry it with you to attract money. Keep the silver bowl and herbs in place until the money is drawn to you.

The Best Time to Do This:

The best time to do this is the waxing moon because it has the ability to help you attract things. Start on the first day that the moon starts to wax. There is no particular month, but it is best to do this at dusk just as the moon is beginning to rise so that you are set up by the time it is up in the sky.

Why These Ingredients:

The silver bowl is pure, and it is representing luck in this spell. You'll find that malachite is green in color, representing money, but it also is known to bring abundance. Cinnamon represents success, and it is also known to draw money. Pine will ward off negativity, and that is why it's used in many money attraction spells. Negative energies can bring bad luck. Dill is used to bring protection and luck as well, helping to attract money. Remember that if you don't have a silver bowl you can use a wooden bowl, but you should purify the bowl beforehand if you have to make this substitution. You can use white sage to purify it, or you can use blessed water.

A Spell for Good Health

Health is a problem for many people. It doesn't matter if you're dealing with undiagnosed medical problems or just the cold, bringing yourself good health is going to help. Health spells aren't a magical cure all, but they'll help to cleanse you of negative energies that may be in the way of you feeling healthier. They will also help to attract good luck to you, which can end up helping to make sure that you get the tests you need on the time that you need to get better.

Ingredients:

1. White Cloth
2. Dried Bay Leaves
3. Carnation Petals
4. Fresh Mint
5. Tiger's Eye Stone
6. White Sage
7. 2 White Candles
8. Blessed Water
9. Fresh Dirt

Directions:

1.   You're going to want to perform this on your altar. You'll need to have your white cloth, and place the two white candles on either side of it.

2.   Next, take your bay leaves, carnation petals and mint. Crush them with a mortar and pestle, and then transfer to a wooden bowl. Add in fresh dirt, and mix with your finger.

3.   Add in the Tiger's Eye stone, covering with the mixture.

4.   Light the white sage, and repeat this incantation. "I call upon the powers that be and all that I know. I call upon Earth. I call upon Fire. I call upon Water. I call upon Air. I call upon Spirit. I ask that you grant me health. I ask that you grant me luck. That I am cleansed of negative energies and the sickness that plague me. I ask the God and Goddess to heal me. I ask the God and Goddess to guide me back to good health. So mote it be."

5.   With that, take a sip of the holy water, and then pour some into your mixture. Wait for the sage to burn out, and then blow out the candles. Take the Tiger's Eye and carry it with you while you're striving to get better. Wrap it in the white cloth.

The Best Time to Do It:

The best time to perform this is under the full moon because it'll give you more time, but this isn't always a possibility. You can use the waning moon to help banish negative energies, but do not do this under the waxing moon. It can bring negative energy to you instead of banishing it. Always make sure that you do this at night when the moon is bright in the sky. You should not perform this when the moon is covered by clouds.

Why These Ingredients:

Carnation petals are great for healing, and they'll dispel negative energies, just like your white sage and white candles. The white cloth is meant to keep it pure, but you can transfer the stone into a medicine bag. Mint is used for the same reasons as carnation petals. Dried bay leaves are used for cleansing negative energies, and you'll find that tiger's eye is meant to help bring protection. It is what you're asking the God and Goddesses to bless so that you can carry it and their power can work through the stone to help heal you.

Beauty Spell

If you're worried about your looks, than this beauty spell is for you. It'll help you to make sure that you look and feel beautiful, so transfer your inner beauty to the surface, and watch as people start to stare. It's an easy, simple spell to use, and there's no bad time to do it.

Ingredients:

1. You'll need a fresh spring
2. 1 Mirror (Silver preferably)
3. Rose Essential Oil

Directions:

1. Go to a stream. It should be fresh water, and then light the rose essential oil.

2. Dip the mirror into the water, facing upward. Let the water rush over it, and close your eyes for just a moment.

3. Open your eyes, and look down into the mirror with the water sill washing over it.

4. Repeat this chant. "To all the powers that be, I ask that others might see, the inner beauty within me. I ask that I look

sweet. I ask that it shows my care. I ask that I may be seen as lovely and fair."

5.   Repeat that chant three times, and then remove the mirror, let it dry as the essential oils burn out.

6.   Hang the mirror in your home, and then look at it twice daily. Look into it before you go to bed, and look at it when you get up in the morning. You should see results within one to two weeks. It may be your hair looking shinier, it may be your teeth looking whiter or skin more fair.

The Best Time to Do It:

It's best to do this as dawn. It doesn't matter the day or the time of the year. Just do it at dawn and outside. The sun should be shining this time, as it is not something that needs to be done by the moon.

Why These Ingredients:

Roses are known to help attract love and show beauty. You can use a different essential oil if a different one speaks to you. However, rose essential oil or jasmine is the most common to work for this spell. They are considered to be feminine, and they'll help to bring your inner beauty out. A silver mirror is preferred because silver will hold the magic better. The mirror will become a channel for the blessing.

Happiness Spell

Happiness usually comes from emotional wellbeing, and that's exactly what this spell concentrates on. You need to be able to put away your stress, anxiety, and all of your worries. It'll help you to calm down, take a breather, and become a happier person by banishing negative energies from your life and your body.

Ingredients:

1. 1 Red Candle
2. Lavender Essential Oil
3. 1 Gold Cord
4. 1 Silver Cord
5. 1 Cord of Your Favorite Color

Directions:

1. Start by lighting the red candle and burning the lavender essential oil. Take a moment to concentrate on your breathing. With each breath make sure that you breathe in positive energy and breathe out negativity.

2. With each breathe you should feel yourself getting lighter, and then you'll take your three cords. Tie a knot on each end, and start to braid it. With this knot say "I release stress and negativity".

3. Keep braiding, and in the middle make one more knot with them all. "I will keep positive."

4. Keep braiding, and at the end make another knot. "Grant me happiness, peace of mind, and joy."

5. Carry this braid with you until you find happiness, and gently blow out the candle.

Best Time to Do It:

There is no one time to do this. You can use the power of the sun or the power of the moon to complete this spell. It's all about personalization, and that means that you need to choose which will be best for you. Dusk or dawn is usually a preference.

Why These Ingredients:

A red candle is meant to represent courage and strength, and fire is meant to cleanse. It's why the red candle is used in this happiness spell, and you'll find that lavender is a stress reliever, and it helps with anxiety as well. Both will help you to bring happiness. Silver and gold represent abundance and luck, and you'll have your favorite color mixed in to tie the spell to you.

Power Spell

There is always some reason that you might want more power, and you'll find that it's easy to achieve power when you have the right spell. It usually requires that you carry something with you.

Ingredients:

1. 1 Leather Bag/Pouch
2. ½ Teaspoon Agrimony
3. Anise
4. ¼ Teaspoon Benzoin
5. ½ Teaspoon Borage
6. 1 Moss Agate

Directions:

1. Take everything but the stone and place it in the pouch, mixing together.

2. Add in the moss agate, and then repeat this chant. "I ask the God and Goddess to grant me the power of will and strength to get through the times to come. I ask that they

lend me their power and their guidance to get through trying times and achieve my goals."

3.   Wear the pouch to lend you strength and power.

The Best Time to Do It:

The best time to perform a power charm is at dusk. It should be right after a full moon, but you can do it any time if you have to. A new moon will be okay as well. Always make sure that the sun is just starting to rise, as this time of change will aid you in your spell.

Why These Ingredients:

Moss Agate is considered a warrior's stone. It's meant to dull pain, strengthen confidence, will power, and improve your health. It'll even help you to reduce your tension and stress. Agrimony will banish negative influences and energies that could keep you from becoming powerful. Anise will raise your psychic power vibrations to the highest level possible when used correctly. This means that I'll help to increase the power of your spell. Benzoin will lend power, and it'll increase your will power. Borage will lend courage and the ability to focus under pressure.

Getting Rid of Bad Habits

Everyone has a bad habit that they want to break, and it can be difficult, but you can ask the God and Goddess to help. There's no reason to keep gambling, biting your nails, or drinking coffee every single day. There's always a way to break a bad habit, and this spell will help you to find your will power to do it.

Ingredients:

1.　1 White Candle

2.　1 Black Candle

3.　1 Green Candle

4.　Clove Essential Oil

Directions:

1.　Before lighting the candles, make sure to anoint them with the clove oil. Place the clove oil around the wick with your finger, and then place them in front of you.

2.　Light the candles, and repeat this chant. "My bad habits will go away, I do not have the time for them during any day. I banish them from my life when all they do is cause me strife. As I will, so mote it be."

3.   Let the candles burn out on their own.

The Best Time to Do It:

The best time to do this is on a full moon, but the moon phase is optional. It is ideally cast right after a New Moon, and it should be done right after Samhain. This is when things are starting to die and new things will take its place.

Why These Ingredients:

The white candle will represent purification. The black candle will represent the death of the bad habit. Green will represent your health growing stronger without the habit. The clove oil is meant to cleanse, and it's a compelling herb that will help to lend you the will power you need to break the habit.

Protection Spell

It doesn't matter what you're protecting yourself from. You need something. It can be protecting yourself from bad energy, bad people, or a physical threat, but protection can help you to become more successful, happy, and stay healthy. A protection charm is usually best, and that's exactly what this spell helps you to create.

Ingredients:

1. Black Onyx
2. Dragon's Blood Essential Oil
3. 1 Teaspoon Rosemary
4. Blessed Water
5. 1 Teaspoon Thyme
6. Silver Bowl

Directions:

1.   Take your thyme and rosemary, putting it into the silver bowl. Then add in your dragon's blood essential oil. Four to five drops is best, and then add in some blessed water.

2.   Repeat this chant. "I am strong. I am safe. The God and Goddess look out for me. They guide me. They protect me. So I will it, so mote it be."

3.   Place the stone into the mixture. Cover the black onyx with it.

4.   Repeat. "I ask that I am guided. I ask that I am protected. I ask that the God and Goddess keep me safe. Lend me your guidance."

5.   Take out the stone the next morning, and keep it with you as a protection token.

The Best Time to Do It:

This is best done on the Aries moon. It's between March 21st and April 20th. This is because the Aries moon will help to bring protection and attraction. Pairing it with the full moon will make it more powerful. Make sure the moon is high in the sky when you begin.

Why These Ingredients:

Black onyx has been used for protection throughout time, and it is because it is meant to clarify your options, defend against negativity, and it sharpens your senses. Dragon's blood is known to expel negative energy and bring positivity into your life. Rosemary and thyme are both protective herbs, and silver will help to keep your intentions for the spell clear. You can also use anise to focus this spell, but it is not required. It will just help to make the spell a little stronger.

Finding Lost Things

Sometimes you just can't remember what you're looking for, and when it's small a simple spell that can be set up easily is always a help. However, you may need a little more time if you're looking for something that's of more importance.

Ingredients:

1. 1 White Candle
2. Pine Essential Oil

Directions:

1. Anoint the candle with the pine essential oil. Burning the pine essential oil while saying the chant is optional.

2. Repeat this chant after lighting the candle. "Goddess please, I am too weak, I cannot find the things I seek. Please help me to locate what I've lost, I've pondered, searched and thought. Bring me the item I desperately need. So I will it, so mote it be."

The Best Time to Do It:

There is no time that is necessary for this spell. However, if what you're looking for is large, such as a lost legal paper, you may need to do so under the moon. Wait until the evening and set up right before midnight for the most energy.

Why These Ingredients:

The white candle is pure, and it is meant to help you look into the flame so that you may speak to the Goddess. Pine essential oil focuses your mind and energy, making it more likely for you to be heard. You can use clove essential oil if you don't have pine, but pine is considered to be easier to get ahold of. Even with these ingredients, it make take a few days to find what you're looking for.

Peaceful Sleep

This is a pouch that is a little harder to make, but it's sure to give you sleep dreams when you're having trouble. You'll need to make sure that you have the time to make it, and it's not something that you come back to. This pouch is even known to help get rid of nightmares because it'll help to relieve stress and release negative energy.

Ingredients:

1. ½ Ounce Sea Salt
2. 1 Pink Candle
3. 1 Silver Candle
4. ½ Ounce Rosemary, Dried
5. 15 Cloves, Whole
6. ½ Ounce Mint, Dried
7. 1 Small Leather Bag

Directions:

1.   All of the ingredients will need put into the leather pouch. Make sure that you have a peaceful state of mind when doing so. Lavender essential oil is meant to help with this if you are having trouble. You need to light all of the candles while you work.

2.   Repeat this while you work. "Sleep well, dream well, and reach peace. I will reach peace. I will have good dreams, and I will find restful sleep."

3.   Place the pouch where you need to, but remember that it needs to be near the bed. It can even be put under your pillow or hung around a bedpost.

4.   You will need to make a new one every three months.

The Best Time to Do It:

Dusk is the best time to cast a sleep spell. It should not be cast during the day or it could cause you to get even less sleep. You do not have to cast this spell in the dark, and you can cast this spell indoors. However, many people say they get the best results when it's cast outside.

Why These Ingredients:

The silver candle purifies, and the pink candle is meant to help you find peace. If you do not have a silver candle, you can use a white one. If you don't have a pink candle, try a green one for good health. Sea salt is purifying, and rosemary and mint is meant to dispel negative energy and provide protection. Cloves will help to focus the energy in the bag, providing you with a stronger spell.

A Peaceful Home

Sometimes all the stress and anxiety that you deal with in your life will affect the energies in your home. It's important that you decrease the negative energy levels in your home to have a happier, peaceful home. Dispelling these energies will help you to feel happier in your house, and it'll once again become a safe haven.

Ingredients:

1. 2 White Candles
2. Lavender Essential Oil
3. White Sage

Directions:

1. Anoint the candles with the lavender essential oil before burning. Put one at the front door and one at the back door.

2. Then take the white sage, and go to each room of the house, repeating this chant. "Bless this house with less stress, bless this house with happiness. Take the negative energy away, and make the positive energy double and stay."

The Best Time to Do It:

It's best to do this just as the sun is breaking over the horizon. Sunrise is better than moonlight because daybreak is known to help purge negative forces and energies, and you can use it to your advantage to cast this spell.

Why These Ingredients:

Sage and white candles are meant to purify. Lavender essential oil will help to relieve stress, and it's known to help lift your spirits and promote positivity. If you do not have sage, you can use Dragon's Blood incense instead since it will purify as well.

Energy Spell

You'll always need a boost of energy here and there, and there's no reason to take an energy drink when you have an energy spell at your disposal. All you need is a candle, and you'll find that drawing from fire is a great way to get the energy that you need to succeed for the day, but remember that it doesn't last long. It'll only help for a few hours.

Ingredients:

1. 1 Red Candle

Directions:

1. You're going to need to light the red candle, and then take a few deep breaths to center yourself. You'll then want to look directly into the flame. Touching the candle is also known to help.

2. While staring into the red candle repeat this chant. "Fire, lend me your energy. Lend me your strength. Lend me what I need to keep going."

3. Repeat three times before extinguishing the candle. Take deep breathes in-between.

The Best Time to Do It:

It's best to do this around noon when the sun is high in the sky, and this is because the sun and the element of fire are considered to be connected. This will give you the most energy.

Why These Ingredients:

The red candle represents fire, energy, and the sun. Staring into the flame while repeating the chant will help you to siphon this energy. If you don't have a red candle, you can use another color, but it won't be as strong. Do not use a black candle for this spell.

Confidence Spell

Everyone could use a boost of confidence here and there, but sometimes you need to make sure that you have the confidence to keep going. This can help in speeches, and it can help when you're trying to apply to a job. It can even help you in school and in stressful situations.

Ingredients:

1. Lavender Essential Oil
2. Dried Chamomile Flowers
3. Clove Essential Oil
4. ½ Cup Sea Salt

Directions:

1. Draw a hot bath, and then mix in your chamomile flowers, lavender essential oil and your sea salt.

2. Take an oil burner, and burn the clove essential oil.

3. As you're mixing everything in, you need to repeat this chant three times. "I am strong. I am beautiful. I am confident."

4.   Then soak in the bath for at least thirty minutes. Let the essential oil burn out on its own.

The Best Time to Do It:

The best time to do it is at night, but there is no particular moon phase. It may give you confidence and relax your body, but when it's paired with a good night's sleep, you're sure to feel confident and ready in the morning.

Why These Ingredients:

Chamomile and lavender are both known to boost confidence and make sure that you erase your stress, anxiety, and negative energies. Clove essential oil is being burnt so that it helps to add power to the spell. However, you'll find that it can be irritating to the skin, and that is why it's being burnt instead of putting it into the water with you. You can use chamomile essential oil if you don't want to use the flowers.

BIG BOOK OF SPELLS

© 2015

An Introduction to Witchcraft

If witchcraft is for you, you've probably already felt a calling towards it. It gives you the power to make a change in your life by calling on the powers that be as well as the power that's in yourself. It allows you to use this energy to manifest what you want or need. You have to embrace witchcraft for it to work because it means you'll open up your channels to accept and direct the energy of the world around you.

Witchcraft is becoming more and more popular, and there is both light and dark magic. However, it is not the magic or spell itself that makes it light or dark. It's all about the intent behind the spell, as intent will guide the energy when casting your spell. You can find spells for health, self-esteem, luck, financial success, and so much more.

Witchcraft can be used for healing, and it is considered to be an Earth based practice. You can practice witchcraft as both a Wiccan as well as a Pagan. Herbs, essential oils, and candles can make the difference. This book will explain when is the best time to perform each spell as well as why the ingredients were chosen. Ingredients don't have to be hard to get ahold of, but you'll find that if the ingredient list is short, then it will usually require more energy. However, less energy is usually required if the ingredient list is long. It all depends on what you feel you have to put into it. Time or energy.

A Simple Love Spell

Everyone wants to find love, and it isn't always easy, but you'll find that with this love spell it's a little easier. It's basic, but it's also powerful as long as you do it properly, so never try to rush it.

Ingredients:

1. Blank Parchment Paper
2. A Normal Pencil
3. Red Tapered Candle

Directions:

1. If you know who you want to love you, then you'll want to write their name on the piece of paper. If you don't know who you want to love you, then write some characteristics of the person you want to love you on the paper. This is usually the safer way to find love, but make sure that it's realistic or your spell will not work.

2. Hold the paper in your hand, and make sure that you focus on that person or those attributes. Put as much feeling and desire into it as you can, and then you can use this chant: "I call upon all powers above, and I ask they hear this call of

love. Like this candle, let it flame and spark, and capture love in their heart."

3.   You'll need to repeat this spell each night for a full week. Then, light the red candle and burn the paper. Bury the ashes in the earth.

The Best Time to Do It:

The best time for this spell is during a full moon. A few days before and a few days after the full moon is best. This will give your spell more strength. It is also best that you do this outside under the moonlight for the best results.

Why These Ingredients:

The red candle is just meant to signify fire, and this represents love, lust, and desire. It'll help you to send your wishes to the powers above. The paper and pencil have no large significance.

Confidence Spell & Charm

Sometimes you don't have enough confidence on your own, and that can be fixed. You'll find this confidence charm will give you the boost you need to be successful, so there's no reason to worry. Make sure that you keep the jewelry on you for it to work.

Ingredients:

1. A Piece of Silver Jewelry
2. 1 Yellow Candle

Directions:

1. You'll need to start by lighting the yellow candle and repeating the following chant: "I wish for confidence, to achieve and do my best…"

2. Take the jewelry and hold it above the flame, and chant: "Now using this charm, help me achieve my best."

3. Then close your eyes, and concentrate on mustering all of the confidence that you can. Then, blow out the candle and take the jewelry with you. You should wear it for it to work.

The Best Time to Do This:

You will want to perform this during the waxing moon, as to bring confidence and good fortune to you. Do not do this under the waning moon, or your spell may not work at all.

Why These Ingredients:

A yellow candle represents yourself, and it's the color of confidence and happiness. It can also represent inner peace. Sterling silver should be used because it reacts well to magic and holds it.

Week Long Luck Spell

You don't always want to do a luck spell for every single day that you need it. If you're going to have a hard week ahead of you, try this wonderful spell to achieve good luck for an entire week.

Ingredients:

1. 1 Silver Candle
2. 7 Pieces of Parchment Paper
3. Black Ink Pen
4. A Silver Bowl

Directions:

1. Take the piece of paper, and all you need to do is write the word luck on it. Writing "good luck" is okay as well.

2. Light the silver candle, and then burn the paper. Drop it into the silver bowl, and let it burn out completely. Meditate while it's doing so, and bring only positive feelings to the forefront of your mind.

3. Do this for seven nights for seven days of good luck.

The Best Time to Do This:

The best time is under the moon, and starting on the full moon is always best. It should be just as the moon is rising into the sky, so right after sunset is always best. However, some people will do it at the witching hour, which is midnight.

Why These Ingredients:

The silver candle is meant to represent good fortune, and the paper and pen are a way of communicating your thoughts and concentrating on what you want. The silver bowl is meant to contain the magic and enhance the spell.

Single Candle Money Spell

You don't always have a lot of ingredients on you, and that's why this is a great spell. You only need something to carve with and a single candle. It's easy to use, and you'll find that it's quite effective if you do it right.

Ingredients:

1. 1 Green Candle
2. A Knife

Directions:

1. You're going to want to carve your name on one side of the candle, and on the other side you're going to carve the word wealth.

2. Next you're going to light the candle, and repeat this chant: "I ask that the God and Goddess bring me wealth and fortune. I ask that I find financial success."

3. Repeat three times, and then blow out the candle.

The Best Time to Do It:

The waning moon is the best time to do almost any money spell, but the best day of the week is on Thursday. Thursday is ruled by Jupiter, and when you cast on Thursday waxing and waning moons don't count as much.

Why These Ingredients:

By carving your name into the candle, you're directing your energy. The green candle represents success, wealth, and financial fortune.

Luck in Finding a Job

Finding a job can be extremely hard for some, but you'll find that this spell will help you to find one a little more quickly. It won't guarantee you get every job, but as long as you do it with the resumes that you put in, then it'll be a little easier. Luck will be on your side.

Ingredients:

1. An Incense Burner
2. 1 Teaspoon Lemon Balm Essential Oil
3. 1 Teaspoon Ginger Essential Oil
4. 1 Teaspoon Cinnamon Essential Oil

Directions:

1. Take all of the oils, and put them together in an incense burner.

2. Write your job application, and then hold it over the burning oils. The wisps of smoke should envelope the paper. You have to close your eyes and envision that the application will be successful.

The Best Time for This:

There is no particular day, but it's best to do this at sunrise. This symbolizes the coming of something new and rebirth. Do this outside during the sunrise.

Why These Ingredients:

Ginger essential oil will represent both courage and valor. It'll help to bring about something new. Lemon balm essential oil will focus and center your energy, and it'll prove cleaner, positive energy towards the spell. Cinnamon essential oil will bring you prosperity in your endeavors, such as finding a job.

A Mirror Beauty Spell

If you don't feel like you're beautiful enough, then you'll want to try this, but make sure that you invest in a good mirror. It can't be something plastic. Getting a metal mirror is best, but silver is preferred if you want it to work properly. The quality of your ingredients will affect the quality of the spell. This is a stronger beauty spell, and it's a little more advanced.

Ingredients:

1. 1 Small Silver Mirror
2. 3 Red Candles
3. Rose Essential Oil

Directions:

1. Light your three candles, making sure you're in a secluded spot. You need to be in your underwear. You cannot have any other clothes shielding you from the God and Goddess.

2. Take the rose oil, and put some on your fingers. You'll then anoint the parts of your bodies that you feel you have a problem with. Then, look towards the moon.

3.	Chant the following: "Goddess of the Moon, please allow your light to make my true beauty shine."

4.	Then, you'll need to transition your gaze into the mirror. Make sure to visualize everything that you want to look like and what you want others to see in you.

5.	Use the mirror to direct the moonlight to where you put the oil.

6.	Perform this spell weekly.

The Best Time to Use It:

You'll want to do this at midnight the first night, and it should be under the power of the full moon. Make sure that every week after it is the same day and around midnight as well.

Why These Ingredients:

The red candle is to represent desire, lust, and sex appeal. The mirror is meant to reflect the moonlight and take in the blessing of the Goddess. The rose essential oil represents love, lust, and beauty. It also represents femininity.

General Luck Spell

If you don't want to use a charm for luck, then you'll find that this is a better luck spell. You can always redo it when you feel your luck waning, and how long the spell lasts is dependent on the energy that you put into it. It will vary person by person, but you can perform this spell as much as you want.

Ingredients:

1. 1 Orange Candle
2. Cinnamon Essential Oil

Directions:

1. Take the cinnamon oil, and then rub it around the wick and the top of the candle. You're anointing the candle with the oil.

2. Now you can light the candle, and you'll want to repeat the following chant: "Powers that be, please listen to me. With no harm to anyone, please let luck come."

The Best Time to Use It:

Wednesday is the best time for a luck spell, as it brings luck and prosperity. You're going to want to do this spell as Wednesday comes into being, so make sure that you do it as the sun is rising. Since you're using sunlight, you do not need to worry about the moon phase.

Why These Ingredients:

Cinnamon oil is going to lend prosperity and power to this spell. The orange candle is meant to focus your energy, and it represents both luck and personal strength.

A Bath for Wealth

Some spells require a simple bath, and you'll find that they're easy and even fun. They'll help to relieve stress, and it'll help to make sure that you have wealth and prosperity in your future as well, so you'll be able to relax and rest easy.

Ingredients:

1. Grated Ginger Root
2. 2 Cinnamon Sticks, Halved
3. Handful Basil, Fresh

Directions:

1. You'll want to run a hot bath like you normally would to relax in.

2. It doesn't matter what order you add the herbs in, but they all need to go into the water.

3. Submerge yourself in the water, but make sure your eyes are closed. You do not need to submerge for long. The cinnamon and ginger can make your eyes burn if you do not keep them closed. You'll need to rinse them out immediately if you experience a burning sensation, and then try again later.

4.   Soak for just a moment before getting out and drying off. These herbs may irritate your skin, and that's why you don't need to stay in for long.

The Best Time to Do It:

The best time is at night, but it doesn't truly matter what time of night. Since it's a money spell, Thursday is usually best.

Why These Ingredients:

Ginger stimulates your energy into taking action, which can bring you wealth. It also helps to purify the body from negative influences. The cinnamon adds power to the spell, and it's known to help with financial success, as previously stated. The basil will harmonize you, but it will also bring wealth and stability.

A Magical Bag for Wealth

This is a more advanced spell for wealth, and it's known to work quicker because of it. It's harder to get right, but when you take the time to perform it properly, then you should get more instant wealth. However, it does not exactly bring success, so this wealth is not considered to be stable.

Ingredients:

1. A leather Pouch
2. 1 Green Candle
3. Cinnamon Essential Oil
4. 3-4 Cinnamon Sticks
5. A Single Dollar Bill
6. Small Piece of Green Cloth
7. Green Ribbon
8. Dried Basil
9. Jasmine Flowers

Directions:

1.   Mix everything together except the cinnamon oil and your candle, and put it into your pouch after lighting the candle. Anoint the candle with cinnamon oil first.

2.   Hold the candle in one hand, and your constructed pouch in the other. Repeat the following chant: "Basil will help to do the deed, and cinnamon will do the trick. I need money fast and quick, so I will it, so mote it be."

3.   Carry the pouch with you.

The Best Time to Do It:

It's best to do on Friday, and it's best on the waxing moon. This will banish misfortune and bad luck, and Friday is chosen because the money is needed for something that will bring your happiness. This can include paying needed bills so that you feel more comfortable and stable.

Why These Ingredients:

You use a leather pouch because it is completely natural, but you can use a cloth pouch as well. You already know that the green candle, cinnamon essential oil, and cinnamon sticks are to bring wealth, prosperity and luck. The green cloth is there for the same reason, and basil brings wealth and luck as well. The dollar bill is meant to focus the energy of the spell. The green ribbon should be silk if possible, as it is considered to be more pure. Jasmine represents courage, happiness, and luck. It can bring prosperity and success.

Home Protection Spell

Bad things can get into your home, and it can affect your negatively. You need to make sure that you protect yourself and your home. This is a simple protection spell that can come with powerful results.

Ingredients:

1. 1 Silver Bowl
2. Spring Water
3. 1 Teaspoon Sea Salt
4. 1 Teaspoon Dried Rosemary
5. 6-8 Drops Juniper Essential Oil

Directions:

1. Mix everything into the bowl, and then let it all soak together under the sunlight for one to two hours.

2. Take the bowl back into your home, and sprinkle the now magically infused water in every room of your house. Make sure to sprinkle it on doorways and windows. Any entrance to your home should be covered.

3.   Repeat the following chant: "I ask the God and Goddess to protect and bless my home. So I will it, so mote it be."

The Best Time to Do It:

It is best to do this every year between August 21st and September 20th. This is the time of the Virgo, and it is the best time to protect your house. Try to do it on a Saturday, as that will help to increase the energy in your spell.

Why These Ingredients:

The silver bowl, as you know, is to enhance the magic. The juniper essential oil is meant to protect, and that's why it's added. Sea salt is meant to purify, and rosemary will help to protect against and banish negative energies. Fresh spring water is usually best because of the purity.

Fertility Spell for a Couple

If you aren't having luck conceiving a child with your loved one, then you're going to want to use this fertility spell. It is powerful, and it does involve blood. You need to make sure that neither of you have a disease that can be transmitted through blood before continuing.

Ingredients:

1. A Knife
2. Red Wine
3. 1 Red Candle
4. 1 White Candle
5. 1 Silver Cup or Goblet

Directions:

1. The female in the relationship needs to fill up the cup with the wine, and then place the red candle to the right of the white one. The male should stand on the left.

2. The female then needs to prick her finger, adding a drop of her own blood to the wine. Then, prick your lover's finger, adding his blood to the wine as well.

3.   The couple needs to chant this chant together: "With this blood, we offer our love. Our intent is to have a child, giving life to another."

4.   Have the male light the white candle, and then he needs to recite the following chant: "I wish to be the father, and I give balance by lighting this candle. I wish balance on me and the mother."

5.   The female will then need to light the red candle, reciting the following chant: "I wish to be the mother, and I light my candle to bring happiness to me and the father."

6.   Next, take the goblet and hand it to the would-be father. "With this silver cup, I call forth our future child."

7.   The male will then need to drink about half of the wine before handing it back to the female. He should repeat the following chant: "With this drink, I call fourth our child."

8.   The female will then drink the remainder, and they both need to chant the following: "So we will it, so mote it be."

The Best Time to Do It:

The new moon will bring forth new change, and it's sometimes best to perform on the new moon. However, others will say that it is best to do this on the full moon and to ask the Goddess of the Moon to bless you. It is up to personal preference. However, the best time of year to do this is around when winter turns to spring. This is December 21st to January 20th. Around the 21st of December is the winter solstice, signifying the death of something and as the time goes the coming of something new. Renewal, and this is the best time for a fertility spell.

Why These Ingredients:

First, you need to know why blood is added. It represents your own life, and your willingness to give your life to another. You mix your blood to show that you wish to bind each other with a child and to another life. Blood carries your energy and your essence. It is powerful, and it focuses all of your energy, tying it together and into the spell. Red wine is an aphrodisiac, and it also represents your life energy. The red candle represents happiness, lust, love, and desire. The white candle represents the purity and innocence of the child, but it also represents the purity in your request as well as peace.

Spell to Increase Fertility

If you're still having trouble or wish to avoid blood, then this fertility spell is for you. It will help to increase your chances of conception, but you may still have to do it more than once.

Ingredients:

1. Sandalwood Essential Oil
2. 1 Gold Candle
3. 1 Silver Candle
4. Lemon Essential Oil

Directions:

1. Take your incense burner, and burn the lemon essential oil.

2. Anoint the gold and silver candle with the sandalwood essential oil.

3. Light the candles after placing the gold on your left and silver on your right. Your partner should be present, and you both should kneel between the candles, facing each other. Close your eyes, and take a moment to meditate and visualize the child you want to have.

4. Open your eyes and blow out the candles together. Then you can try to conceive. You will need to do this every time that you try to conceive until you have a child.

Best Time to Do It:

There is no best time to do it. This is for conception, but if you know you are ovulating, this will only increase your chances of conception.

Why These Ingredients:

The silver candle is meant to channel and increase the energy put into the spell. The gold candle is meant for appositive influence, and it will help to bring fortune and luck in conception. Lemon essential oil is also known to bring fertility and luck. It is also meant to cleanse. Sandalwood essential oil is specifically for conception and fertility in this spell.

An Amulet of Happiness

Sometimes happiness is harder to achieve than you want it to be, and that's where this amulet will come in handy. It'll help to sort out negative energy and bring more positive energy into your life. It will also help to relive stress and anxiety.

Ingredients:

1. A Silver Charm
2. Silver Bowl
3. 1 Teaspoon Sea Salt
4. Dried Lavender Flowers
5. Marjoram Essential Oil
6. Rain water
7. 1 Blue Candle
8. Cinnamon Essential oil

Directions:

1. You're going to want to mix your sea salt, rain water, dried lavender flowers, and marjoram essential oil into a bowl.

2.   Take the silver charm, and place it into the bowl. Set it out during the day, and then take it in at nightfall. When the moon rises, go back out with the candle and cinnamon essential oil.

3.   Anoint the candle with the cinnamon essential oil. Then light it.

4.   Repeat the following chant: "I ask the powers that be for peace and happiness, I ask that I am guided and I am blessed. So I will it, so mote it be."

5.   Take out your charm, and then run it through the flame, visualizing happiness. Blow out the candle, and meditate under the moon with your charm in hand.

The Best Time to Do It:

The best time is a full moon, as it'll give you the most power. If you can, try to also do so on a Friday, but it may not be possible. If it lines up, always use this date because it is meant to help bring happiness as well.

Why These Ingredients:

Cinnamon oil is to increase the power of your blue candle, which represents happiness. Use royal blue if you can, as it will work best to increase your happiness. Do not use indigo. The silver in the bowl and charm will hold the magic. The sea salt will purify and remove negativity, and the lavender flowers are going to relieve stress and anxiety that is plaguing you. Marjoram essential oil is meant to bring happiness and peace.

A Protection Pouch

This pouch is something that you should carry with you if you're feeling like something bad is going to happen, but you can use it any time. It's a powerful protection charm, but you need to make sure to keep it on you for it to work.

Ingredients:

1. 1 Leather or Cloth Pouch
2. 1 Tigers Eye Stone
3. Myrrh
4. Dried Parsley
5. Sea Salt
6. White Sage
7. Silver Bowl
8. Rain Water
9. Dried Rosemary

Directions:

1. Take the rain water, and place it in your bowl. Next, add in your rosemary and sea salt. Place your Tigers Eye in it.

2.   Burn the white sage beside it, and let it soak in the sun until nightfall. It's best to do this near dawn so it has all day.

3.   Take it out, and let it dry. Light more white sage to purify it, and then once it's dry you can assemble your bag.

4.   Place all remaining ingredients in the bag with the Tigers Eye on the bottom. Carry it with you.

The Best Time to Do It:

It's best to do this under the full moon for more power, and the light of the moon will help to protect you and purify your bag. However, do not do this near the witching hour. It lets too many things around you while making your pouch.

Why These Ingredients:

Your pouch needs to be natural, and the Tigers Eye is in there because it represents strength and protection. Myrrh is added because it also helps to protect and channel spiritual energies. Parsley also offers protection, and it cleanses negative influences and energies from your person. Sea salt is also added to purify negativity in the water. The dried rosemary will offer protection from negative energies as well as spirits.

A Good Dream Pouch

You won't always have good dreams, and when nightmares start to plague you, this dream pouch will help. It'll help to cleanse your dreams, relive anxiety and stress, and it'll help both children and adults. It's easy to assemble, but it does require a lot of ingredients.

Ingredients:

1. Cloth or Silk Pouch
2. Chamomile Flowers, Dried
3. Lavender Buds, Dried
4. Rosemary, Dried
5. Anise, Whole
6. Lepidolite Stone
7. Sea Salt

Directions:

1. Place everything into the pouch together, and repeat the following chant: "Nightmares that plague me, leave me be. By the power and strength, set me free. So I will it, so mote it be.

2.   Seal the bag, and then place it near your beside. Many people find that it helps more when you place it under your pillow.

The Best Time to Do It:

It is best to make this during the day because you're already having problems at night. Friday is the best day to make it because it is meant to bring peace and happiness.

Why These Ingredients:

Chamomile flowers will help to relieve your depression, stress, and anxiety that might be causing your nightmares. They will give you inner peace. The lavender buds are added for the same reason, and the rosemary is meant to purify and bring peace and happiness. Anise is meant to provide better channels for sleep, banishing nightmares. Lepidolite promotes a calm state of mind, and it helps to solve any sleep disturbances. The sea salt makes sure that the stone is purified with no negative energies. Soaking it in salt water beforehand will also help.

Say Goodbye to Stress Spell

Stress can get in the way of your happiness, and that's why it's important to get rid of stress and negativity. This spell will cleanse you, and it'll give you a pouch to carry around to keep stress away. Stress can lead to anxiety and depression, and that's why it's important to get rid of it quickly.

Ingredients:

1. Bayberry
2. Chamomile Flowers
3. Witches Grass
4. Ylang Ylang Essential Oil
5. Apatite Stone

Directions:

1. Burn the ylang ylang essential oil in your incense burner.

2. Then take your pouch, and start to put each ingredient into it. Before putting the stone in, hold it in the middle of your palm. Repeat this chant: "I ask that stress leave me be, I ask that the God and Goddess set me free. I ask that my

worries disappear, I ask that my future is clear. Please bless this stone, and bring me peace."

3.   Place the stone into the bag, and seal it.

Best Time to Do It:

The best time to do this is the new moon, as it is the moon of new beginnings. It will allow you to let go of all of your stress and start anew without too much cleansing being necessary. Keep the bag on you at all times for the best results.

Why These Ingredients:

Bayberry is known to relieve stress, and it can also be called Waxberry or Candleberry. Chamomile will also release stress, and it'll help to promote emotional healing. Witches Grass will relieve depression, and it'll help you to promote happiness. Burning ylang ylang oil will relieve your depression and stress, and it promotes a calm and peaceful nature. Apatite stone is a blue stone, and it gives an uplifting energy frequency. It'll help with inner wisdom as well, and it'll help you to bring a sense of peace and calm to your life.

Simple Banishing Powder

Powders can have magical properties as well when you infuse them with magic, and that's exactly what you're doing when you're creating this banishing powder. It'll banish negative energies, and it'll make sure to protect your home as well. There are steps, and for it to work, you can't skip a single one.

Ingredients:

1. ½ Cup Sea Salt
2. ¼ Cup Black Pepper
3. 2 Teaspoons Cloves, Ground
4. 2 Teaspoons Thyme, Dried
5. White Sage

Directions:

1. Before you mix anything, take the white sage and light it. You'll want to open up every door and window. Go to each room and entrance way, and repeat the following chant: "Evil spirits leave me be, you're not welcome in my home. Let this smoke purify and cleanse. Let it banish negativity and sin. So I will it, so mote it be."

2.   Afterwards, mix your remaining ingredients together to make a powder, and then sprinkle it over each entryway to your home. Leave it undisturbed for three hours.

3.   Take your broom, and sweep it out, but don't worry about taking everything with it. It's okay for traces to be left behind.

Best Time to Do It:

It's best to do this during the day, as negative energies and spirits are weaker. However, if it can wait, you'll want to do this at least once a year. Do this during the time of the Virgo, which is from August 21st to September 20th.

Why These Ingredients:

You already know that sea salt purifies, but black pepper is known to banish. It's also a protection against evil spirits. Cloves are going to banish and protect from negative spirits as well. It raises the vibrations in an area to a healthier more spiritual one. Thyme is also meant for banishment as well as purification, so it'll work well when mixed with the other ingredients. White sage will help to purify the area before you put down your powder.

A Spell to Stop Procrastination

The act of procrastinating can become an addiction or habit, and it's something you need to break to gain any success. This spell makes it a little easier, but it does require your will power to work. The energy you put into it will determine how quickly and strongly this spell works.

Ingredients:

1. 3-6 Drops Lemon Essential Oil
2. 1 Tablespoon Sweet Almond Oil
3. 1 Red Candle

Directions:

1. Mix your lemon essential oil with your sweet almond oil. Anoint your forehead, wrists, and neck.

2. Light your candle. Inhale the smell, and gaze into the flame. Repeat the following chant: "I can do better. I will do better. I ask for guidance, and as I will it, so mote it be."

3. Meditate under the moonlight until the candle burns out.

The Best Time to Do It:

It's best to do this under the full moon, but other than that there is no particular time that this is best. It's best to do this every month until procrastination is no longer a problem.

Why These Ingredients:

Lemon essential oil is going to help to give you a clearer sense of your goals. It's meant to remove what's blocking you as well. Sweet almond oil is supposed to help you break addictions, bad habits, and it provides a sense of calmness. The red candle is meant to represent your self-determination.

Spell to Purify an Item

When you get an item secondhand, then you'll want to purify it to make sure that nothing negative comes with it. This is one reason you'd want to purify an item. If you are getting a bad feeling from any item in your home, then you should purify it as well. Always trust your gut.

Ingredients:

1. Cedar Chips
2. Silver Bowl
3. Rosemary Needles, Dried
4. Thyme, Dried
5. Sage Leaves, Dried

Directions:

1. You need to put the cedar chips in a bowl, and then you need to light them. Once they smoke, add in your other ingredients. Everything should catch fire, but you may need to give it a minute.

2. Pass the items through the smoke while repeating this chant: "Rosemary, sage and thyme, I ask that you remove any

negativity and evil that may be within. Cedar clear this energy, and renew it again. Smoke, I ask that you wash away its past. As I will it, so mote it be."

3.   Wait for everything to burn out naturally.

The Best Time to Do It:

The waning moon is best since the waxing moon increases things. The waning moon decreases things, helping with banishments and cleansings. Tuesday is best because it ruled by Mars, and it helps you to fight off negativity.

Why These Ingredients:

Cedar chips will give you protection, purification, and it also represents healing. Rosemary will get rid of the negativity that may cling to the item, and thyme is common for pacification as well. Sage removes negative energy in general.

Healing Ritual Bath

Healing can sometimes need a helping hand, and you'll find that's exactly what this spell does. All you have to do is soak in a relaxing hot bath after preparing it. It's really that simple, but always keep in mind that you'll need quality ingredients for it to be effective.

Ingredients:

1. 6-8 Drops Eucalyptus Essential Oil
2. Spearmint Leaves, Fresh
3. Yarrow Flowers, Dried
4. Agrimony, Dried

Directions:

1. Draw a hot bath, and then add in everything. Make sure that it's mixed throughout the water.
2. When it's all mixed, make sure to soak for at least twenty minutes. Then you can get up and dry off.

The Best Time to Do It:

Sunday is ruled by the Sun, and it'll help to increase your bath. You should do this at night when you can let go of your worries and relax. The waxing moon will help to increase your healing vibrations.

Why These Ingredients:

Eucalyptus is meant to help attract healing vibrations that will help to speed up the healing process. Spearmint will help with stress as well as healing, and it's easy to get ahold of and grow in your own garden. Yarrow flowers will ward off negativity while also increasing healing vibrations. Agrimony will overcome any inner blockages which can keep you from healing as well.

A Spell for Headaches

Headaches can hit anyone, anywhere, and there's no reason to always turn to over the counter medication to get rid of them. A spell will usually work, but remember that belief matters or you'll block your energy flow. You'll find that you don't need many ingredients for this spell to be quick and effective.

Ingredients:

1. Lavender Essential Oil
2. 1 Smokey Quartz Crystal
3. 1 Rose Quartz Crystal

Directions:

1. You're going to want to wash both crystal sunder water first, and then put them in the sun for several minutes so that they charge.

2. Put the lavender essential oil into your incense burner, and light it so that it burns.

3. Make sure you're in a quiet environment, and breathe in and out slowly, but also breathe deeply. Take the stones, holding the rose quartz in your left hand. It emits peaceful

vibrations, and you'll want to hold the smoky quartz crystal to your forehead. Imagine that it absorbs the pain.

4. Continue until your headache is gone.

The Best Time to Do It:

You need to do this during the day because the stones need to charge with sunlight to be effective for healing. However, you'll find that there is no time of day that is better than another.

Why These Ingredients:

Rose quartz emits calming and healing vibrations, and therefore it is commonly used to heal minor ailments such as headaches. Smokey quartz crystal is meant to absorb negative energy, and you can use it to absorb pain. The sunlight charges with a healing light, and that's why you need to charge them with the sun. Lavender essential oil is meant to relieve stress, which can help to reduce headaches in tension.

A Bedside Spell for Health

Health is extremely important, and this health spell doesn't require too many ingredients to cast. It's easy to cast, and it'll help a lot during cold and flu season.

Ingredients:

1. 1 Onion
2. Chia Seeds
3. Spring Water
4. Coriander Seeds
5. 10 Drops Eucalyptus Essential Oil

Directions:

1. Cut the onion in half, and place it in a shallow, clean dish. The cut half should be open. Place it by your bedside.

2. Add a little spring water, but it shouldn't even cover half the onion. Add in all other ingredients. Chant the following: "With these ingredients, I ask that my health increase. With these words, I wish for my stress to be relieved. With this spell, I ask that I become healthy again."

3.   Let it sit overnight. Change it out every night before bed, and you should notice that you grow a little healthier by the day, and it'll help you to recover quicker as well.

The Best Time to Do It:

The waxing moon is best because it'll help to increase your health, but you can do this at any time without much effect from the moon. Starting on Tuesday is best because it'll help to banish whatever is causing you to become ill and stay that way.

Why These Ingredients:

An onion is known to gather negative energy, including illness in the air. It'll help to protect you against these energies. Chia seeds are also known to help with health as well as protection. Spring water is used for the purity. Coriander seeds are also for health, and it has the added benefit of promoting peace. Eucalyptus oil will promote healthy vibrations, as stated before.

Digestive Health Tea Spell

Tea can help you, but when you cast a spell over tea, it's much more likely to help. It won't just help that once, either. It'll help you to make sure that you stay healthy and that the tea will have a stronger effect.

Ingredients:

1. 8 Ounces Water
2. 2 Teaspoons Honey, Raw
3. 1 Teaspoon Chamomile, Dried
4. ½ Teaspoon Anise
5. 1 Teaspoon Lavender Buds, Dried

Directions:

1. Start by brewing your tea. You're going to need to boil the water, and then add in your anise, lavender, and chamomile. Let steep for six to eight minutes.

2. Strain, and then add in your honey. Stir well, and as it cools, put your finger around the rim, and go around it three times. Repeat the following chant: "With this tea, I ask for

health. With this tea, I ask for relief. With this tea, I ask for health for me."

3. Then drink the tea before it goes cold.

The Best Time to Do It:

The best time to perform this spell is whenever you are having trouble. However, it usually works better at night when the moon is high. This is a spell you can use whenever you need it.

Why These Ingredients:

Honey is known to actually help with your digestive health on its own. Chamomile will help with healthy vibrations and calming your stomach. Anise is known to purify and calm the stomach. Lavender will relieve stress and relax your muscles.

A Spell for Decisions

A spell for decisions may seem silly, but everyone has a hard time making decisions from time to time. It's meant to clear your thoughts and give you a little more drive to succeed, so don't worry if you go into it without a clear idea of your outcome. That's exactly what this spell is for.

Ingredients:

1. Blank Parchment Paper
2. A Pen
3. 1 Grey Candle
4. Silver Bowl
5. 1 Teaspoon Sweet Almond Oil
6. 3-5 Drops Bay Laurel Essential Oil

Directions:

1. Take the parchment paper and write down the question you're having a hard time answering. Remember not to make it vague. You need to use this to focus your mind as much as possible. Fold the paper in half.

2.   Take the sweet almond oil and mix it with the Bay Laurel essential oil. Anoint your wrists, forehead and neck with the mixture.

3.   Light your candle and repeat the following chant: "With this question, I ask for the guidance of the God and Goddess. I ask that the fire cleanse my mind and clear my thoughts. I ask that I am guided down the right path so as to make the right choice."

4.   With that use the grey candle to light the paper on fire, and then drop it into the bowl. Meditate until it burns out completely, and then blow out the candle repeating this chant: "So I will it, so mote it be."

The Best Time to Do It:

Wednesday is the best day to do this spell, since it's the day where spells with messages work best. It's ruled by Mercury, which is considered to be the planet of communication. Dusk is the best time of day.

Why These Ingredients:

Your parchment paper and pen gives you a way to focus and concentrate your mind. The grey candle should never be silver. Grey is meant to take away confusion and anything that is blocking you from making a decision. The sweet almond oil will clear your mind and bring health, but it is also a carrier oil to keep the essential oil from irritating your skin. The Bay Laurel essential oil is mean to help clear your mind of confusion, helping you to make a decision with clear thoughts.

Henna Tattoo for Attraction

Attraction can be hard, and it's different than love. It's attract to both your physical and mental self. It's a great way to get people to notice you, and you'll find that it's easy to do right. Make sure it's all natural henna powder if you want it to work.

Ingredients:

1. Henna Powder
2. 2-3 Drops Jasmine Essential Oil
3. Spring Water
4. Pinch Nutmeg
5. Wooden Bowl
6. Henna Bag

Directions:

1. Take your henna powder, and place it in the bowl with nutmeg. Add in your jasmine essential oil and spring water until you get a thick paste. Scoop into the bag.

2. Write the word "love" over your heart, and then let it dry while meditating over what you want. Keep a solid

thought in mind such as "I want love", "I want to be attracted", or "I want more positive attention".

3.   Let it dry completely before gently wiping the henna mixture away, and you should have a temporary tattoo that will help you as long as it is there.

The Best Time to Do It:

Do this on Wednesday, as it's the best day to perform relationship magic. Do it under the waxing moon to increase attraction.

Why These Ingredients:

Henna will attract love, but only if it's worn close to your heart. It can also provide you with protection against evil. Jasmine essential oil is another great way to attract love and general attraction to your inner self. Nutmeg when used in small amounts shouldn't irritate your skin, especially when mixed with henna, but it is a powerful herb of attraction. The wooden bowl is neutral as well as the spring water.

Remove Envy & Jealousy

Everyone gets jealous or envious here and there, but it's easier to get over it when you have a little help. You need to cleanse your own aura and energies if you want to get over negative emotions, and it'll free your mind so that you can be successful and happier in your life. Envy and jealousy work as a block that will only keep you from true happiness in life.

Ingredients:

1. Nettle
2. Mortar and Pestle
3. Ground Cloves
4. Basil, Dried
5. Sea Salt
6. Spring Water

Directions:

1. Take all of your ingredients, and grind them into a powder with your mortar and pestle. While making your powder, repeat this chant: "By the God and Goddess, I ask that I be cleansed. I ask that these emotions that plague me wash away. I ask that I remain positive and in your light."

2. Once they're ground, take the powder and wet it, scrub your hands and arms with it, and then wash it away with the spring water. Repeat the following chant: "With these herbs, I ask that they protect and guide me away from the negativity that I feel. So I will it, so mote it be."

The Best Time to Do It:

Under the full moon will give you the best results because it is where the moon is at its peak. It is with this that you get the power you need to cleanse yourself, and it is here then your aura can be renewed.

Why These Ingredients:

Nettle is known to purify you of negative emotions, such as envy and jealousy. Cloves are also known to get rid of jealousy that you feel and clear your aura. Dried basil helps you to move on from negative thoughts and paths to a better one. Sea salt makes sure that nothing is clinging to you that could cause these emotions to return quickly.

Curse Prevention Pouch

If you feel like you're in danger, then you need to protect yourself. This pouch is specifically to prevent someone from placing a curse on you. It takes time and effort, but the ingredients aren't as hard to find as you might think.

Ingredients:

1. Cloth or Leather Pouch
2. Fennel Seeds
3. Anise
4. Bay Leaves, Dried
5. Barley
6. Knife

Directions:

1. Take the bag, and start to fill it with the fennel seeds, anise, bay leaves, and barely.

2. Before closing the bag, take your knife and prick your finger. Allow two to three drops of your blood to fall into the bag. Repeat the following chant: "With my blood I ask that my strength protect me. With this bag, I ask the God and

Goddess lend me their guidance through the dark paths that lie ahead. I ask that with my own strength and their wisdom that I stay safe. So I will it, so mote it be."

3.   Close the bag, and keep it on you at all times. When you are done, burn the bag and its contents. Do this after a month no matter what.

The Best Time to Do It:

The best time to perform this is at midnight on Saturday. Saturday is ruled by Saturn, and this is meant to decrease. That's why it works so well with banishment and protection. It'll get rid of the negative energy, and it's best to perform it on a clear night where the moon is high in the sky.

Why These Ingredients:

Fennel seeds are specifically used to keep curses from being placed on you, and they're great for spells because they also provide general protection and cleansing. When paired together, the anise and bay leaves are meant to cleanse and protect, which will help with curses. Barley is also meant for protection, and it'll keep you safe. Your blood imbeds your aura to the pouch, which is why you need to be careful not to lose it. You're using your own energy to protect yourself.

A Bath for Spiritual Energy

When you're casting spells, you'll want to have as much spiritual energy as possible to put into it. This bath is meant to be a simple spell that is more of a ritual to increase your spiritual energy, giving your spells a boost.

Ingredients:

1. Handful Fresh Mint Leaves
2. Handful Fresh Sage Leaves
3. ¼ Cup Lemon Juice
4. ½ Cup Sea Salt

Directions:

1. Run the bath like you normally would, and make sure that it's hot.

2. Add in all ingredients to the bath once it's drawn, and soak for twenty to thirty minutes. You can then get out and dry off. Meditate while in the bath. Repeat this mantra: "I am cleansed. I am powerful."

The Best Time to Do It:

Thursday night is the best time to use this herbal soak to increase your energy because Thursday is for increasing. It'll help to purify your energy naturally as well.

Why These Ingredients:

Mint promotes energy, and it'll help to increase your energy naturally as you feel rejuvenated. Sage leaves will make sure that the energy you gather is purified, and the lemon juice will revitalize you. Sea salt isn't just for cleansing, but you'll find it's great to ground your energy as well. Grounding will help to renew your energy, helping to make sure that your energy is clean and new.

A Spell for Self-Esteem

Self-esteem will help all other spells as well, and you'll find that this spell will help you in anything that you do soon after. With self-esteem, you'll find that you're a little more grounded and happier as well. It can even relieve stress.

Ingredients:

1. Musk Incense
2. 1 Brown Candle
3. Dried Yarrow Flowers
4. Small Cloth or Leather Pouch
5. Parchment Paper
6. Silver Bowl
7. Pen
8. Cedar Chips
9. 1 Teaspoon Dried Ginger

Directions:

1.   Start by burning your musk incense and lighting your brown candle. Take a moment to breathe in and out, starting to center yourself.

2.   Take the parchment paper, and write down what you want to change. For example, you can write "I will no longer be afraid of myself", "I will no longer fail in my endeavors", "I will no longer have self-hatred". Burn the piece of paper, and drop it into the silver bowl. Let it burn out.

3.   Start to fill the bag, and then add in the ashes of the parchment paper when it's complexly burned up. Tie the bag while repeating the following mantra: "By these ashes, I will grow. By these herbs, I will be stronger. By my will, I will be a better, happier me. So I will it, so mote it be."

4.   Close the pouch, and keep it on you.

The Best Time to Do It:

Do this during the day on Sunday to make sure that you have an increase in your self-esteem and magical energy. It's ruled by the Sun, and it's best to do it around noon.

Why These Ingredients:

You'll find that musk will naturally increase your self-esteem, and it'll help to lift negativity from you, cleansing your energy. A brown candle is meant solely for self-confidence and self-esteem. Yarrow flowers are great for self-esteem as well as courage. Cedar chips are also for confidence, but they also represent power. Ginger is also empowering, as it represents power and success.

A Good Luck Coin

This is a ritual spell, so there are little to no ingredients. You'll find that this is an old spell, and it has Celtic roots. It's important that you have a wishing fountain around if possible, but a moving stream will work as well. Just make sure that the water is not stagnant when throwing it into a large, natural body of water. Natural bodies of water are usually best.

Ingredients:

1. A Single Penny

Directions:

1. Take the penny in your hand. It can be one that you already have, or it can be one that you find. Then, hold it in your hand before raising it to your heart, concentrating on the following mantra: "This penny is for luck." Take a moment with your eyes closed, concentrating only on this. Repeat it to yourself.

2. Move it from your heart to where your third eye is located, which is in the middle of the forehead. Repeat the mantra again, and then kiss your hand that's holding the penny.

3.   "Give this penny to the spirits for luck." Is what you'll need to say as you throw it into the moving water, and then you're going to need to walk away. Don't look back.

The Best Time to Do It:

This is a daytime spell, so you're going to want to do it on Sunday since it's ruled by the sun. You do not perform this spell by moonlight, so try to keep it before dusk. Dawn will also increase the power of this spell. However, the next best time to do this is at noon. However, if you look for a day to increase, you can also use Thursday, since it'll increase the power of the spell. It's also known for luck spells, but since this is a ritual, Sunday is still the recommended day.

Why These Ingredients:

The penny is just meant to represent the fortune that you currently have, and it's used because it is a relevant currency. If you are outside the US, us something else.

A Little about the Power of Belief

Belief will make a difference when you're casting a spell. You need to believe in what you're doing, or you're going to set up a mental block that will keep the spell from working. Spells rely on your own energy infusing into them to invoke even the God and Goddess blessing you, so you need to be able to let that energy out. A way to do that is through belief. Without it, you'll find that nothing happens at all.

When you start to believe negative things, these things will come true. This can be especially true when dealing with spell work. You need to learn to clear your mind and keep a positive line of thinking at least when casting the spell. A great way to do this is to meditate before you try and cast a spell, pushing all negative thought away from yourself so that the spell will be successful.

Keep away from these thoughts:

- "I can't do this."
- "I am not a healthy or lucky person."
- "I am unable to do better than this."
- "I will never find love."
- "Money is the root of evil, so this won't help."

- "Bad things always happen to me."
- "I'll never be happy."

These are the thoughts that will keep spells from working because you have a block in your mind. You will not be able to transfer any energy into the spell with thoughts like this present. Instead, turn these thoughts positive so that you increase the amount of energy you're releasing, and this way you're much more likely to get the results you want from your spells.

About Intent & Desire

This can be just as important as making sure that you believe in what you're trying to cast. If you don't have the desire or the right intent, then this will block the spell as well, and to have the right ones you have to understand these concepts. The entire purpose behind a spell is to give you a way to manifest something that you feel you want or need. Intent is a vital part of your success. You need to want what you're doing badly. You need to know what you're trying to accomplish clearly. You need to know exactly what you're seeking as far as an outcome is concerned.

Most people will actually define their outcome automatically, and so the hardest part is sometimes recognizing that you have one defined. Bring it to the forefront of your mind so that you see it clearly while casting the spell. Many of the coincidences that people experience is the manifestation of intent without the need to cast a spell, so there's no reason to write it off. Magic does exist in everyday life.

Your desire needs to be clear in your mind as well. Make sure that your passion for what you're doing shows in your spell work if you want the energy level to increase. Without desire or passion, your spell is either extremely weak or void completely. So it's best to make sure you understand and want a spell to work before you try to cast one.

Some people find that defining what they want is easier when they have it written down, but as you start to get used to channeling your energy, you'll find that this isn't necessary. However, if you're having a hard time with casting spells and seeing result, trying writing out your intent and desire before you start. Define it clearly, and it'll help you to keep those thoughts in your head. You can also repeat it like a mantra for better results if you are having a hard time focusing and concentrating.

Printed in Great Britain
by Amazon